Social Work with Coloured Immigrants
and their Families

edited by J. P. TRISELIOTIS

Social Work with Coloured Immigrants and their Families

Published for the
Institute of Race Relations, London
by
OXFORD UNIVERSITY PRESS
LONDON
1972

Oxford University Press, Ely House, London W.1

GLASGOW NEW YORK TORONTO MELBOURNE WELLINGTON
CAPE TOWN IBADAN NAIROBI DAR ES SALAAM LUSAKA ADDIS ABABA
DELHI BOMBAY CALCUTTA MADRAS KARACHI LAHORE DACCA
KUALA LUMPUR SINGAPORE HONG KONG TOKYO

ISBN 0 19 218404 0

© Institute of Race Relations 1972

*Printed in Great Britain
by Ebenezer Baylis and Son Limited
The Trinity Press, Worcester, and London*

It's coming yet, for a' that,
That man to man the warld o'er
Shall brothers be for a' that.

Robert Burns, 'For the Sake of Somebody'

Preface

The primary aim of this book is to help social workers provide a more effective service for their coloured immigrant clients. It has been designed to meet the practitioner's need for a closer understanding of the tensions and pressures arising out of immigration and of the implications of socio-cultural factors for the social work process. Until recently, there has been an over-reliance on psychodynamics to the neglect of sources of knowledge from sociology and anthropology which could be useful for social work.

The articles chosen for this publication draw mainly from socio-cultural concepts, and aim to alert social workers to certain possibilities that may necessitate a change of approach and a modification of traditional social work methods. As with white British clients, in work with immigrants the choice of method and goals, as well as the direction of treatment, is heavily dependent on an accurate psychosocial diagnosis. Such diagnosis, however, presupposes a good grasp of the reality of the immigrants' world, including the impact of past and current experiences. This knowledge should help social workers to recognize in what ways coloured immigrant clients are the same as or different from their customary white British clients, and whether specific behaviour is cultural or symptomatic of pathology.

Though some of these articles have previously appeared in journals, there has been a persistent demand from practitioners for a publication that would bring together what little material is available and make it easily accessible for quick reference. The editor's original intention was to include articles demonstrating a variety of social work methods, but that was not possible because of the limitations imposed both by the availability of material and the actuality of current

viii *Preface*

practice. Social work with coloured immigrants is a subject around which very little is known and very little has been written, possibly because immigrants have for too long been a fringe interest of too many workers and because of the small size of the coloured population until the 1960s. The important implications of a differential diagnosis for social work were perhaps underestimated. It is hoped that starting from this preliminary identification of certain processes and practice observations, social workers will contribute further towards the development of new knowledge about working with people from different ethnic backgrounds. No detailed material about individual cultural backgrounds has been included here, as this has been so admirably done in Robin Oakley's *New Backgrounds: The Immigrant Child at Home and at School*.[1]

It is recognized that when writing about the implications of social work with coloured immigrants from different ethnic backgrounds, a number of generalized points, conclusions, and hypotheses are inevitable. In a small publication of this kind, there is a need to find a common denominator that will accommodate all the major characteristics, recognizing at the same time that many of these views and hypotheses have still to be critically investigated in greater depth and detail. We can only speculate at this stage how the first-generation immigrants, and especially their children, will be further affected by life and conditions in Britain. Social work cannot be practised without regard to people's new experiences and, especially, to the quality of such experiences. Some of the methods suggested in this volume may be found to be irrelevant to subsequent generations. There is a growing need to understand the developing sub-culture and outlook, especially of the young. Current public and official attitudes will have a great bearing on how far the children of the first-generation immigrants come to feel that they belong here.

Although this book has been predominantly planned with social workers in mind, the information should be of relevance to other caring professions outside the social work field.

The first article, by the editor, looks at the coloured immi-

1 Published by Oxford University Press, London, for the Institute of Race Relations, 1968.

grants' socio-cultural backgrounds and their relevance to the social worker in his attempts to reach a differential diagnosis and set appropriate goals. It also examines how certain social work methods can be adapted or given a new emphasis to meet the immigrants' psychosocial needs. Bessie Kent considers the possible areas of cultural conflict in work with immigrants and gives an analysis of British middle-class attitudes.

The article by Juliet Cheetham describes some of the main difficulties faced by the coloured immigrant community in this country and the problems faced by social workers who are trying to help them. Gus John's contribution is from a more individual sociological analysis. He writes about young blacks as individuals who may have special problems and needs and who react against a system that is ascribing to them a low status and is trying to define them as a problem.

June Ellis contributes on 'The Fostering of West African Children in England'. This is a well-documented socio-anthropological study which aims to provide some insights into West African life and should help social workers towards an understanding of the needs and attitudes of West Africans, mainly student-parents, seeking foster-care for their children in this country. Dr. Stewart-Prince sensitively examines the mental health problems of pre-school West Indian children and identifies some of the contributory social and emotional factors. The final chapter, by the editor, tries to bring together some of the ideas expressed earlier and discusses some relevant current issues.

Finally, I should like to thank the editors of *Alta*, *Social Work*, *Social Work Today*, and *Maternal and Child Care* for their prompt permission to reprint some of the articles that appear in this book.

Edinburgh University   J. P. TRISELIOTIS
1971

Contents

Preface vii

I The Implications of Cultural Factors in Social Work
with Immigrants 1
J. P. TRISELIOTIS

II The Social Worker's Cultural Pattern as it Affects Casework with Immigrants 38
BESSIE KENT

III Immigrants, Social Work, and the Community 55
JULIET CHEETHAM

IV The Social Worker and the Young Blacks 78
GUS JOHN

V The Fostering of West African Children in England 91
JUNE ELLIS

VI Mental Health Problems in Pre-school West Indian
Children 102
G. STEWART-PRINCE

VII Conclusions 109
J. P. TRISELIOTIS

Select Bibliography 121

I | The Implications of Cultural Factors in Social Work with Immigrants

J. P. Triseliotis[1]

Social workers in Britain are becoming increasingly aware of the importance of knowing about the socio-cultural background of their clients, especially those from different ethnic groups. Earlier attitudes, such as 'immigrants are different and therefore we cannot understand them', or 'they are like us and there is nothing more to know', led to a failure to attend to their real needs. To offer help of personal nature to immigrant clients the social worker must know not only in what ways they are different or similar to the local people, but also how the various ethnic groups differ amongst themselves. The implications of such knowledge for practice are obvious: the choice of method and the setting of goals are dependent upon a differential diagnosis. No accurate diagnosis can be arrived at, however, without a good grasp of the background socio-cultural influences and of their implications for social work practice.

It is now recognized that human behaviour and the development of personality are greatly influenced by socio-cultural factors. The values, traditions, and standards of a culture strongly influence the functioning of a family and through it the development of its individual members. A sense of self-image and identity is cultivated from the moment the young infant begins to recognize another face, progressing to gradual identification and assimilation of other confirmatory experiences about his own parents, ancestors, people, country, and its history. This is the material on which identities are based. The 'I' of the present is an accumulation of all the 'I's' of yesterday and yesteryear and can only be

[1] Dr. Triseliotis is a Lecturer in Social Work and Social Administration, Department of Social Administration, University of Edinburgh; formerly, he was a psychiatric social worker in North London.

I

understood in the context of country, relatives, origin, environment, among other factors. Societies also assign roles and tasks to individuals, compatible with the culture, within which they can recognize themselves and feel they belong. To be a real person presupposes a basic identification and trust, first in one's parents and then in one's culture. Because culture is internalized from childhood, it is very difficult to change, but it is not static either. Though immigrants change their physical environment, they do not necessarily change their cultural character and cultural identity. The tenacity with which immigrants here have been holding on to attributes that are indivisible parts of their cultural and self-identity, has led us to a re-examination of the concept of assimilation and integration. It is now recognized that an appropriate goal for policy-makers and some others (although the social realities of what, in fact, happens are more complex) is for the toleration of cultural diversity and the acceptance of cultural pluralism. The most appropriate definition given on integration is that of the ex-Home Secretary, Roy Jenkins, who in addressing a meeting of Voluntary Liaison Committees said: 'I define integration not as a flattening process of assimilation but as equal opportunity, accompanied by cultural diversity in an atmosphere of mutual tolerance.'

This should not prevent individuals from any ethnic group from integrating and absorbing certain values and traditions of another culture that are found to be compatible and enriching. A sense of personal and social security, however, appears to be necessary before an individual can positively integrate new influences without having to refute any or the whole of his background. Even under ideal conditions, new-comers in any area take some time before they feel emotionally ready to seek relationships outside their own group and to participate in the life of the local community. No doubt this process can be accelerated if appropriate programmes are set up in an atmosphere of acceptance and toleration. Original cultural traditions and values become most important to people, like immigrants, who feel less secure and, frequently, rejected. When minority groups struggle for their existence against the local majority, which either rejects or threatens to stifle them, they desperately try to hold on to their differences and to things that are familiar. But it is this retention of individuality that is often criticized and attracts a fair amount of scapegoating from the local community. The latter suddenly discovers an obvious group on to which it can transfer many of its prejudices.

Experience from practice suggests that a display of strong ambivalent feelings about one's original culture and home country, may be an indication of similar feelings towards parental figures. The lack of a positive identification with parents usually leads to a lack of cultural identification. In treatment people affected in this way may strongly deny feelings of homesickness or sadness arising out of their recent losses. Some may try prematurely to shed their past, and may uncritically over-identify with the host culture. The value, however, of integration which arises from self- and cultural alienation is very doubtful. Subsequently, this alienation is likely to extend to the newly adopted culture.

Hopes and Disappointing Experiences

Because of the separations involved, immigration has many similarities with death, but by its very nature it also implies a strong belief in change. In many respects it has an optimistic side about it which contrasts sharply with the general fatalistic attitude that is usually found among coloured immigrants in this country. They have a strong belief that you cannot change the course of nature or of events and that everything has been determined in advance by supernatural forces. 'Everything has been and will always be.' These attitudes may reflect feelings of chronic weakness and the ever-present lack of political power. For the same reason, immigrants tend to see most of their crises as externally induced. The strong belief in the supernatural that some immigrants display can easily be mistaken for signs of psychotic behaviour. For instance, mental disturbances (mostly acute delusional or manic states or acute depressive reactions) are viewed as caused by evil powers 'outside' of the individual and manifested in different forms ('fairies', 'the evil eye', 'black magic'). Curative measures again may include a mixture of quasi-magic, quasi-religious practices.

Before they embark for their trip to Britain, these same people build unrealistic hopes of a better future. (Possibly they would never have embarked on the journey if they did not have such high hopes.) Their high expectations are often reinforced by letters from relatives and friends, who, in their wish to present themselves as a success, exaggerate greatly the positive aspects of life here. After the first weeks of honeymoon are over, the new-comers have to reconcile their expectations with the often harsh reality that surrounds them. This coincides with the period when the depression arising from the loss of relatives, friends, and country catches up with them. Given time and some sympathetic understanding from those around them, the depression will lift and they will also begin to accept their new situation and start to think about the future. This does not necessarily stop them from feeling homesick and sad, but it is an indication of their personal strengths that they can tolerate such feelings without having to deny them or be paralysed by them. For a few, however, this can become a lasting preoccupation with all its incapacitating effects.

As the decision to emigrate is usually based upon a wish for betterment, it is not surprising to find that achievement and success assume priority value among the new-comers. Emphasis on success gives rise to an amount of individualism which is uncharacteristic of an aspect of most immigrants' background—the tradition of support and sharing. This is a revelation which greatly surprises new immigrants, when they fail to obtain the customary support from relatives and friends. The great pressure to succeed, which is very much reinforced by pressures from the home country, is usually underlined with the fear of failure and its accompanying shame. It is the lack of success and the fear of 'losing face' that often prevents a great number of them from returning to their home countries. Added to this is the serious shortage of jobs back home, as well as envisaged problems of readjustment.

Though many West Indian immigrants come from urban areas, a large proportion of immigrants, and especially those from India and Pakistan, come predominantly from peasant areas. Life and institutions in the countries of origin are organized in ways that prepare the individual to cope with life situations within that society and not with the urban and technological problems faced by countries like Britain. The environment in which they grow up does not favour, for instance, the development of elaborate concepts or complex decision-making. Only a limited vocabulary is used, and imagination and abstract thinking are less well developed than among people reared in Western societies. The peasant background from which most immigrants come favours a rigidity of roles. There is usually a specialist for every job such as carpenter, cobbler, mason. There is no do-it-yourself attitude or tradition. The flexibility of role that is required here, i.e. doing things about the house or looking after children, can cause considerable conflict. In general, however, most immigrants are people with considerable personality strengths and resources. They are loving parents and husbands wanting to work and improve themselves.

Back home the child at first, and the adult later, are mostly exposed to and are in touch with a more simple but tangible world of real things. Similarly, they are mostly occupied out of doors, which favours movement and activity rather than abstract thinking. There is more activity and doing, whilst talking is concerned with a more tangible type of world. Because of this, the children generally develop a very poor vocabulary and are limited in their sentence construction and in the variety of tenses used. This kind of background can lead to educational difficulties for the children who emigrate to Britain where the emphasis is on verbal communication and imaginative thinking. Bernstein[1] has drawn attention to the role of speech as a major aspect of culture and as an important means of the transmission of culture from generation to generation. Most of the immigrant children will never have set eyes on a toy, or painting or drawing material, or any children's books. In fact, some children need to be taught how to play. In many respects, immigrant children have more in common with local children from deprived neighbourhoods. As immigrants mostly gravitate towards deprived areas, their children's handicaps are correspondingly increased. The lack of environmental stimulation and

[1] B. Bernstein, 'A Socio-linguistic Approach to Social Learning', in J. Gould (ed.), *Penguin Survey of the Social Sciences* (Harmondsworth, Penguin, 1965).

the poor educational, nursery, and other facilities can hardly help either the immigrant or the local child.

Any social services that exist in the countries from which most immigrants come, are of a rudimentary kind. Social work, with few exceptions, is an unknown activity, and the notion of a professional relationship alien to their cultures. There is no welfare stereotype, either good or bad. Priority needs after arrival are mainly connected with housing and employment and then education for their children. There is no tradition of asking for or receiving help with personal or emotional problems from people outside the family and especially from public agencies. There is widespread ignorance about the purpose of the social services and of their complex organization. No planned effort has ever been made to explain the services to immigrants, possibly because of fears that they might then over-use them. The school, which is the most familiar institution to immigrants of every nationality, has hardly been used as a place to establish contact with them and introduce them to some simple aspects of British life.

Other writers have highlighted the fact that the way in which social and public services in general are organized here, often acts as a deterrent to their use. To a large extent, these services can only be used by people endowed with considerable perseverance and personal strengths. If this is, in fact, true for indigenous members of the community, it must be even more daunting for immigrants who are much less familiar with the operation of the services and who are more vulnerable to criticism. Because of these difficulties, immigrants come to rely heavily on relatives and friends for advice, as well as sometimes depending on the services of unscrupulous fellow-countrymen. Once immigrants get to know about the social services, they are likely to use them without many inhibitions. The new-comers have no experience and memories of the thirties, of means tests, or of any assumed stigma attached to the users of the services. In this respect, they are free from the emotional connotations and undertones of such stereotypes as 'employment exchange', 'assistance', 'welfare'. British society, however, is of two minds about whether it wants immigrants—or, for that matter, local people—to use the various services. At the same time that conferences are being held to find out why immigrants do not make better use of the social services, fears are being expressed about the exploitation and heavy demands that immigrants reputedly make on the services. Antipathy towards coloured immigrants may have complex psychological roots, but there is a tendency to rationalize it in economic terms, which are often contradictory. Thus people argue that immigrants take jobs from white workers; that they have a higher tendency to be unemployed and are, therefore, a burden on the social services; and that they keep down wages in jobs where they are found in the largest numbers. Also, it is believed that they use up hospital beds, houses, and school places which would otherwise have been available for the locals. A recent evaluative analysis of *The Economic Impact of Commonwealth Immigration* by Jones and Smith[1] suggests that on balance the standard of living of people in this country has risen more with the presence of Commonwealth immigrants than it would have done without them. It is often forgotten, too, that the country benefits considerably from the fact that the first-generation immigrants are mostly people in the prime of their working life who have not been supported here whilst at a dependent young age.

The majority of immigrants experience their first major hardships and disappointments when searching for employment and accommodation. The P.E.P. report[2] revealed that discrimination against coloured immigrants is substantial and that because of racial prejudice immigrants have the jobs lowest in status and pay. A recent report by Rees,[3] published by the Runnymede Industrial Unit, claimed that racial discrimination can occur in industrial employment even where it is contrary to the policy of higher management. Rees examined employment policies and practices at a brewery, a furniture factory, and a gasworks, all in London. Coloured workers, he reports, were finding it unreasonably difficult to get jobs and when they did, they were excluded from better

[1] K. Jones and A. D. Smith, *The Economic Impact of Commonwealth Immigration* (London, Cambridge University Press, for National Institute of Economic and Social Research, 1970).

[2] Political and Economic Planning and Research Services Ltd., *Racial Discrimination* (London, P.E.P., April 1967).

[3] T. Rees, *Policy or Drift* (London, Runnymede Trust, 1971).

paid work. Top management might say that all workers were to be treated equally, but line managers were left to hire, dismiss, and promote. No positive or effective steps were taken to see that they observed the personnel policy which had been laid down. Things were left to drift, and the drift was in an unequivocally bad direction. At the gasworks, for example, the assistant engineer said that coloured men were not wanted for skilled jobs; they would be hired only for the jobs that white workers would not do. This, in effect, meant the rougher and dirtier unskilled work.

Though the Race Relations Act 1968 has a key function in checking racial discrimination, there is yet no evidence that it has made real inroads. The annual report for 1969–70 of the Race Relations Board makes two important points about this matter. In paragraph 95, the Board states: 'Though we believe the passage of the Act and its enforcement by the Board have had an impact, we also believe that unlawful discrimination . . . remains substantial.' The Board also says (paragraph 70) that: 'The real remedy is for employers to recognize their obligations under the Act and to take action to eliminate discrimination.' If employers widen opportunities for suitably qualified immigrants, this will itself help towards some dispersal in housing and the avoidance of immigrant islands in a number of cities. Whilst the first-generation immigrants may be content to accept menial jobs that are generally not wanted by the white British, the real test of race relations will come when their children who have been brought up and educated here, begin to look for jobs. It is unlikely then that they will be satisfied, unless the jobs and other opportunities open to them are commensurate with their qualifications. If no solution is found to this problem, we will observe the phenomenon of 'under privilege' identified exclusively with race. This situation will force the young coloured generation to polarize its feelings on the question of race.

It is well known that housing is very scarce and that large numbers of white families are in as desperate need of better housing as are many immigrants. Immigrants, as a group, tend to go to places where there is employment available, but these are also the areas with acute housing shortage. Because of their low income and racial prejudice, they are driven into the worst housing conditions. The only accommodation they can obtain is in twilight and decaying areas from which everybody wants to get out. They live in overcrowded conditions, with little space and few facilities either in their homes or in the neighbourhood. They can only go where they are wanted, but they are only wanted in places where most other people do not want to go or stay. Although they have little choice where they go to live, they are exposed to a double-bind type of criticism: they are criticized for concentrating in large numbers in certain parts of the big cities, for threatening to take over these areas, and for not dispersing. This is in spite of the fact that opportunities to disperse are constantly denied them, very often by the people who criticize them.

The P.E.P. report of April 1967 supplied evidence of widespread discriminatory practices—some deliberate—among local authorities. In *Housing on Trial*, Burney[1] came to the conclusion that: 'West Indians and Africans get a raw deal not because of any outright Council policy to victimize them, but because countless small decisions are made by jelly-kneed and narrow-minded minor officials.' She goes on to say that housing managers make assumptions about black men being dirty, or their inability to get on with white neighbours. And when Africans or Indians live in slum houses, they tend to be left to the remotest phases of redevelopment plans because of all the administrative difficulties of coping with streets full of overflowing houses. Burney argues that 'no amount of legislation will really work as long as so many people in key positions in the field are so patently biased in their attitudes'. In the case of estate agents and private house-holders, there is fear, ignorance, and the self-perpetuating belief that the presence of coloured residents will depress property values. These attitudes affect mostly Indians and Pakistanis who, because of the special value they attach to home-ownership, try to buy their own houses. The way income is pooled within these families, makes it easier for them to buy a house. This recent comment by an Indian

[1] E. Burney, *Housing on Trial* (London, Oxford University Press, for Institute of Race Relations, 1967).

illustrates the attitude of his countrymen towards home-ownership. He said, after being rehoused by his local Council following a slum clearance programme: 'I cannot live in other people's houses.' Eventually he started looking round for a house to purchase. Jones and Smith maintain that as far as housing is concerned, immigrants have probably been responsible for an improvement in the standard of living of the white population. Their savings have been used to buy houses—often at more than the market price—and have smoothed the move of the indigenous population to the suburbs.

There is little doubt that many coloured immigrants experience disappointments and hardships. Some of the hardships arise out of the general process of adaptation to new situations, and others from the impact of discrimination against them. Feelings of rejection and insecurity are reinforced by hostile political speeches or Press comments. As a result, they tend to withdraw both physically and emotionally, seeking the support of their own and avoiding unnecessary physical or emotional contacts with the local community. The lack of contact, which is reciprocated by the host community, makes impossible any real understanding of each other's way of life and instead generates mutual criticism of differing customs. Immigrants, especially from India and Pakistan, are very critical of English habits of thought and behaviour: for example, eating habits which pay no regard to the concepts of 'pure' and 'impure', but only to those of 'clean' and 'dirty'; the lack of reticence, as typified by behaviour at public meetings; the freedom of the young; and the indiscriminate mixing of male and female in pubs and clubs. They view this society as uncaring, coarse, and 'immoral'; and see themselves as generous and honest. Similarly, the British are critical of the immigrants' eating, dress, religious, and other habits, and look upon those from the East, particularly, as too disciplined, traditional, and rigid. One might recall the famous episode in Herodotus (iii. 38) about the horror expressed by Greeks and Indians at each others' funeral customs. One big difference among the major groups of immigrants, is that the cultural gap between the Indians and Pakistanis and the local English population is deeper and thornier than that between the West Indians and the English. The West Indians who, for historical reasons, lost many of their original cultural values and traditions, came to see some aspects of the British way of life as their own, or something to aspire to, and are, therefore, readier to understand and tolerate certain British forms of behaviour and thought. In contrast, immigrants from the East, who have a firm cultural identity of their own from which they derive their habits and other aspects of their life-style, find many aspects of life here distasteful. Equally, many English people feel an equivalent distaste for the behaviour and habits of Indians and Pakistanis. Though expressions of hostility and rejection cause bitter memories to all immigrants, Indians and Pakistanis, who have a firm cultural identity to fall back on, appear to be less affected than West Indians, who are less fortunate in that they feel rejected by the very culture they have been brought up to see as their own.

What colour prejudice and colour discrimination are doing to black people is illustrated by a few examples that have recently come to notice: A West Indian mother, on meeting her daughter at London Airport, refused to accept her, saying that her own girl was not so dark when she left her in the West Indies. She insisted that this was an 'inferior girl' because of her darker colour. In a number of Children's Homes, coloured children were found scraping their skin in the hope that the black would disappear. Other children would constantly ask their house-parents whether they could turn white in adult life. Others were heard blaming their parents for making them black. A number of children who lived with white foster-mothers, identified so strongly with them that they became very prejudiced against other coloured people and refused to play with black children. Similarly, when some coloured children who were cared for by white foster-mothers returned home, their family saw them as peculiar and different. The norms and traditions of the host culture which had been imposed on the children were seen by their parents and siblings as deviant behaviour. Thus, in placing coloured children, or the children of any other minority group, the social worker must consider two needs: first, that the children be placed in the neighbourhood from which they come; and second, that their foster-parents share the same cultural background as their natural parents. If these two needs are satisfied, the foster-child will be much more able to find his identity. Placement in a distant neighbourhood and with white people increases the immigrant child's feelings of rejection by its parents and by its cultural background. It is important that resources should be made available to explore the possibilities of finding foster-homes among the immigrant population. Perhaps one of the positive contributions of the Black Power movement has been the strengthening of black people's identity by fostering a pride in their colour and in their original culture.

The Presentation of Need

In work with immigrants it is useful to develop a fair amount of understanding about the methods previously used by the individual or his group to cope with particular situations of need or stress. The vast majority of new-comers are people with good ego strengths, but the process of uprooting and resettlement exposes them to multiple pressures that overtax their immediate coping resources. Caplan's[1] analysis of crisis has some relevance to first-generation immigrants provided the worker enters the client's cultural system. A serious threat to the self is posed by the loss of loved ones, and the need to cope with new surroundings and new situations. All these problems result in considerable stress; but given immediate and appropriate support, most immigrants will gradually use their own strengths to deal with them. Intervention on the here and now when the crisis sets in can help to prevent social or psychological breakdown and to ensure better future management of crises.

At this early stage, practical needs generate many problems, but they also divert the immigrants' attention from personal difficulties. If they are referred, or refer themselves, as clients, they will focus mainly on their social rather than personal needs. Because they are mostly people with good coping resources, support in the form of explanation and

---

[1] G. Caplan, 'An Approach to the Study of Family Mental Health', *U.S. Public Health Reports* (Vol. 71, No. 10, 1956), p. 1027.

some concrete help, if necessary, will enable most of them to start using their own initiative and independence. Those who are isolated from relatives and friends may need more concentrated support. It has been observed from practice that immigrant clients tend to present themselves as excessively dependent at first. As British culture attaches a high value to independent functioning, there is a real danger that the immigrants' apparent excessive dependency may either frighten social workers, who may then try to avoid it, or appeal to them so that they cherish it. The amount of dependence displayed, however, is usually temporary and not unrealistic in view of the number of adaptations which have to be made within a short period. Dependency may take the form of needing to be escorted to the bus stop, the employment exchange, the school, or the clinic. Some immigrants will have difficulties with landlords or with schools, social security, or housing authorities. In these circumstances, social workers must be prepared not only to act as their spokesmen, but, where necessary, to represent them at tribunals or protect them from officialdom. Feelings usually take care of themselves when enough interest is shown in helping these clients along with real needs and anxieties and in providing physical services and resources. Experience again suggests that newcomers are more accessible to measures intended to alleviate pressing social needs than to help aimed at resolving interpersonal relationships. This is a time when they need direction and guidance, and efforts to involve them in self-examination and discussions about reaching their own solutions to their problems, may throw them into further confusion. It is the immigrants' initial perception of the agency as caring and helpful that will encourage them to return, if necessary, for help with personal difficulties.

This is not to say that all the immigrants' problems are material ones or simply a matter of adaptation to the British culture. Personality problems exist underneath practical ones. The outward overlay of material problems may often conceal family dysfunctioning, marital difficulties, personal unhappiness, or poor parent/child relationships. The process of immigration affects traditional family functioning and raises conflicts with regard to roles, relationships, obligations, and expectations. The stability of marriage, for instance, is no longer supported by the tight Indian, Cypriot, and Pakistani home communities or by the strong moral force of public opinion. Marital disharmony can be more openly expressed here, and separations and cohabitations become more frequent. There are already signs indicating that not only the functioning of the family unit is adversely affected through the process of immigration, but also the supportive role of the extended family. The family unit is affected by realignment of roles and relationships, whilst the extended family is not usually established here.

The already weak West Indian family appears to be the first to experience the disruptive effects of immigration. Common-law marriages, cohabitations, and other informal arrangements are now more prone to break-up, leaving behind a great amount of suffering and unhappiness. As a result, many West Indian mothers may seek reception into care for their children. Some of the pressure for such requests may be connected with the need to work and support children and other members of the extended family left behind. On other occasions, the children may be beyond the mother's control. It is possible that, as a result of experiences in their home country, some West Indian parents confuse reception into care with boarding-school education; others see themselves as failures and look to state institutions to provide what they feel they themselves cannot provide; in many other cases, reception into care represents the lending, for short or long periods, of external ego-strengths to help them survive unmanageable responsibilities. Recently a lot has been said about the great number of West Indian children who are being received into the care of local authorities. No mention has been made, however, of the plight of West Indians living in appallingly overcrowded conditions, with no facilities such as hot water, bathroom, space to play, or gardens to sit, and with no neighbourhood facilities. In addition, there is no money for proper residential or day-nursery care, or private foster-care. Social deprivation as a factor contributing to family break-up and to emotional and intellectual deprivation has been underestimated. Social workers too, influenced perhaps by the traditional supporting role of the extended family in the West Indians' home country, often place undue pressure on the family or on relatives to cope, at a time when they may be unable to do so. When reception into care is refused, mothers often resort to private fostering or to daily minding. The parents rarely receive help from the social work services in their efforts to make alternative arrangements, and not infrequently some very unfortunate private placings occur. In this respect, it would be true to say that the social services have not yet geared themselves to offering a service to people who cannot be strictly classified as needy under the present rigid classification system.

Problems of interpersonal relationships often come to light through the immigrants' children. The latter may display difficulties resulting either from stresses at school or from pressures within the family. The child's attempts to adjust to an unfamiliar educational and social system frequently lead to learning and behaviour difficulties. Education authorities, with few exceptions, have been very slow in developing flexible programmes that could help to integrate the immigrant child within the educational system. A further difficulty for the children is that parents often try to fulfil unrealistic ambitions through them. All immigrant groups value highly those aspects of the British educational system which they see as an avenue to success. In spite of their professed belief in heredity, they also believe that the child can achieve educationally if he tries hard enough. Contradictory comments are often being made: for example, 'he can't do much, if he hasn't got it in him'; or, 'he can make it, if he only tries harder'. Very high ambitions have been noticed particularly among Indians and Cypriots. Some parental expectations will obviously be fulfilled, but the focusing of exaggerated hopes on the child can become an important diversion from parental anxieties about personal failure or inadequacies. Children generally resent having to become avenues for their parents' expectations. Some of them are kept at long hours of homework, or are expected to stay in to read out-dated and irrelevant books. To my comments on this, many West Indians would reply: 'this behaves him and he also learns'. Children who were so restricted and deprived of environmental stimulation presented a picture of dullness and lack of initiative. They had few facilities at home and the parents, though expecting a lot, provided very little support. Such subjects as music and painting, and such activities as playing, were seen as irrelevant to the child's needs. Excessive pressures, reinforced by other adverse experiences, often resulted in learning difficulties, truancy, and problems of control. Behaviour difficulties are more readily displayed at school where the adults are more tolerant than those at home.

The immigrants who have settled in this country are forced, by circumstances, to live according to the unfamiliar pattern of a nuclear family which makes great demands for self-dependence. Parents, for instance, have no outside contacts and interests and are often isolated. Because of this, both parents, but especially the mother, try to obtain most of their emotional satisfactions from their children. These demands on the child are usually increased if the father spends a great part of his leisure time with his men friends at immigrant clubs and cafés. The mother is left in the cold without the traditional dropping-in of relatives and neighbours or the social activity at the doorstep or the village well or tap. As a result, she consciously or unconsciously does not want to let the child grow towards independence. Many mothers often express direct and indirect anxieties about losing their children. These anxieties take the form of forbidding a child to play with local children, keeping it away from school on slight pretexts, or expressing open hostility if an older brother shows signs of breaking away. The child's use of the English language can often make the mother feel cross and cut off. Children who sense their mother's unhappiness and emotional dependence on them, can feel guilty after their efforts to break away. Because of their long period of dependency, they lack the necessary personal resources to achieve independence without family support.

In spite of the trail of unhappiness left behind them, interrupted family relationships are a common phenomenon of the emigration process. One of the most frequent patterns is for one or both parents to emigrate leaving the children in the care of grandparents or other relatives. The children may join them after any number of years. The pattern with Indians and Pakistanis is for the father to come first and then for children of employable age to follow, before the mother and younger children do so. When children join their parents, the interrupted physical and emotional ties take a long testing time before they are re-established. In some cases, trust will never be reinstated. Many of the West Indian children who come to join their parents are experiencing their second separation: the first occurred when their parents originally left them; and the second, when they left their grandparents who were looking after them. Many of these children are very sad and depressed about leaving grandparents with whom they have had a very warm relationship. The initial lack of trust and the testing-out behaviour that they display here, often generate considerable anxiety and sometimes anger in the less secure parents. Some West Indian parents become very intolerant and even punitive towards children who are being difficult in this way. There is a failure to understand their children's unhappiness, and they cannot accept that the children either missed them when they left the country, or are now missing their grandparents. By the time some children join their parents, other siblings or half-siblings have been born, or the father or mother is living either alone or with a different man or woman. A great number of immigrant children, mostly West Indian, who are referred to social agencies for behaviour difficulties or for being beyond control, have a long history of separation. It should be stressed again that, where the parents react sensitively and with understanding to the child's problems, such an explosive situation is generally never reached. In these cases, the trauma of separation is healed through a new experience that tolerates testing-out and initial mistrust.

The Relevance of Background Knowledge to the Social Work Situation

One of the main contributions of social work practice to the development of the profession is the social worker's ability to reach accurate assessments of social situations. The choice of method and the outlining of goals largely depend on an accurate assessment of the psychosocial situation. The same applies equally to work with immigrants. Most of the social work methods, outlined in social work literature, are also appropriate in work with immigrants. Some methods, however, may have to be adapted or given greater emphasis in certain directions, in order to take account of culturally determined differences and tendencies, as well as the immigrants' particular prevailing value system and their current life situations. Some of these differences can be grouped under the following headings: 1. the pattern of relationships within the extended family and the surrounding community; 2. male-female relationships; 3. parent-child interaction; 4. the expression and significance of feeling; and 5. the concept of time and events.

1. *The Pattern of Relationships within the Extended Family and the Surrounding Community*

The closely knit and cohesive Indian and Pakistani family group contrasts greatly with the more loose and open West Indian family. In the first case, roles and behaviour are rigidly defined; in the second, they are still in the process of being defined. In their home countries, the Indians and Pakistanis generally live in large extended families. Relationships are based on, first, a cohesive family unit, followed by the extended family of relatives and friends, the neighbourhood, the village, and perhaps the linguistic group. The family is a social unit headed by the eldest male and it includes all the brothers and sisters as well as their own children. Within this extended family unit the emphasis is on family ties and obligations. Along with the family, the outside community exercises considerable control and authority over individual attitudes and behaviour. Religion, too, has a pervasive influence over the whole of people's lives. The individual internalizes family group and community controls, and his primary allegiance is to the extended family group. There is a consensus of values and the strict control of the individual is seen to be exercised in his interest. The individual is important only in so far as he contributes towards the importance and well-being of both the family and the community. Any success that he achieves is seen to reflect on the prestige of his family group and his community. In such communities, everybody knows everybody else, and one can feel important to many people, but equally shamed before many people. The actions of each individual are under the scrutiny of all the others. The main satisfactions also come from within the family and the community. With such a background, one usually finds strong ties among siblings and relatives, hence the efforts to send for relatives and friends as soon as possible. It is a way of life, however, that encourages both inter-dependency and prolonged dependency for the younger members of the family. Ambivalent feelings which have no opportunity of being aired before emigration, are more likely to find expression once the process of immigration sets in and the extended family begins to lose its hold. Such feelings are often mixed with a considerable amount of guilt regarding the ones who have been left behind or 'deserted'.

The lives, attitudes, and behaviour of first-generation immigrants here are still extremely influenced by, and are in many respects under the control of, events back home. Unlike the West Indian and Cypriot semi-extended family group which can tolerate a fair amount of dissension and disagreement, the more closely knit Indian and Pakistani groups do not openly admit to internal conflict and differences. Open dissension and conflict are neither encouraged nor tolerated. Differences are strongly denied, and bad feelings are mostly projected on to other neighbouring communities or linguistic groups. The strong cohesion of these families, however, does not easily show signs of dysfunction and disorganization, and it gives the appearance of a well-functioning and mentally stable community. It is a pattern that, because of its considerable strengths, tends to absorb difficulties, and it primarily encourages the seeking of help from within the extended family group, rather than from without. This may partly explain why few Pakistani and Indian families are referred, or refer themselves, to social agencies here. Though they may some-times seek help for social problems, there is no tradition for seeking help with personal, and especially with intimate, problems. Intimate feelings are not, in fact, discussed even within the family. When help is sought on personal or social problems, it is usually an indication that there is very serious family disorganization and that the problem has reached a fairly advanced stage when no easy solution is in sight. Perhaps also because of the strong cohesion and influence of the kinship group, few boys from these backgrounds reach the Courts or are referred for being beyond control. Reception into care is rarely requested, except in situations of extreme crisis. The long-term effects of immigration on this type of family life remain to be seen. Because all members of the extended family, as well as the surrounding community, share in each other's problems and pleasures, social workers here need not have any reservations about including the wider family in their plans and discussions. The immigrants are used to sharing with many people. This partly explains the great isolation that immigrants here experience when in institutions such as hospitals, convalescent homes, and children's homes. Isolated from their own community, often with no knowledge of the language, and feeling misunderstood, they can quickly become depressed and apprehensive. The concept of community care, important as it is for local people, is vastly more so for members of minority ethnic groups who find themselves in institutions of various sorts. Aspects of confidentiality, which are so scrupulously observed with local families, are of less importance to immigrants. Sharing and support are much more cherished than privacy and confidentiality. The whole extended family could be seen as the client, provided the worker follows the correct procedure. With Indians, Pakistanis, and Cypriots, the worker may have to start with the senior male member, thus acknowledging his authority in all external matters. In the first contacts, it is very likely that wives and other female members of the family may take no part in discussions and perhaps not even be present, whilst uncles, cousins, and other male relatives may actively participate.

The West Indian pattern of family life was at first dictated to them by their plantation masters. Following Emancipation, West Indians generally tried to model themselves on the expatriate Britishers and absorbed some of the values and standards of Western middle-class society. The West Indian family type still lacks structure, tradition, and cohesion. It is weak and loose when compared with that of the Indians, Pakistanis, and Cypriots. It does, however, contain many of the features of an extended family. A household in the West Indies could consist of a grandmother, the grown-up single sons and daughters, a daughter's illegitimate child, and perhaps a cousin or a niece whose parents are dead. The grandmother and mother are the most stable part of the family, whilst the father is a more elusive and often absent figure. The effect on the children of the absence of a stable male influence, within the West Indian household, is still to be established. In households which lack the presence of a grandmother, which is not unusual here, the children may experience a very disorganized childhood. They may be passed from mother to stepmother or stepfather or other relatives, and sometimes go into care. For these and other reasons enumerated earlier, the West Indians are less able to contain their difficulties and are most likely to seek help or be referred for support. They are possibly the most vulnerable group among the immigrant population. They have identified themselves with a culture which proves to be predominantly rejecting and discriminating, and their negative experiences generate considerable mistrust towards the host country and towards its public agencies. Because of their tendency to display 'good' manners when in contact with authority figures, their real feelings may be underestimated. As a group, however, they also have their own prejudices towards people from other parts of the Caribbean and may not respond, for instance, to requests for help to care for children from another island.

Whilst there is some evidence indicating that the cohesive Indian and Pakistani family is being threatened and challenged both from within and from outside, some cohesiveness is beginning to emerge in the West Indian family. There is evidence to show, for instance, that West Indians here are increasingly conforming to British norms and values of marriage.

2. *Male–female Relationships*

Among the Indians and Pakistanis, and to some extent among the Cypriots, there is a considerable cultural taboo on sex and on the discussion of intimate feelings. Sexual intercourse is

generally shrouded in mystery. Women must disguise their
sexual attributes, and are almost expected to be sexless. Contacts between members of the opposite sex are greatly dis-
couraged. It is shameful for a girl to attempt to provoke the
desire of a man. Indian and Pakistani boys and girls are
segregated from early on, and girls are not expected to go out
of the house alone or even to meet in their own home men to
whom they are not related. (University-educated people are
generally allowed more freedom, and are excused if they
break sex, food, or drink taboos.) Sexual morality is heavily
repressive. An encounter with a member of the opposite sex,
which may be entirely innocent, can nevertheless be regarded
as an act 'shaming' the family. The girls are generally
expected to be diligent, prudent, and passive, and to attend
to duties ascribed to them by the male-dominated culture.
Most marriages are arranged and the woman frequently pro-
vides a dowry. Her position is subordinate to that of the man.
Men have rather ambivalent feelings towards women whom
they mainly value as child-rearers. These attitudes and customs are carried on, almost unchanged, in this country.
There is less feeling attached to the marital relationship,
whose success is mainly judged on the husband's ability to
provide for and support the family, and not on the sexual
relationship. 'Romantic' love as an ideal is scorned or ridi-
culed. Because the marriage is based on economic considerations, it is far less likely that the husband will fall for another
woman.

Among the marital partners—and this is especially true of
Indians and Pakistanis—there is no tradition of talking
things out, sharing decisions, or having common interests.
Neither is there a tradition of sharing past life situations. The
relationship between husband and wife is somewhat diluted,
in that the husband often looks to his own family as the next
of kin and the wife may look similarly to her own father or
mother. There is a rigid division of labour with definite pre-
scriptions of what a man or a woman can or cannot do. Inter-
changeability of roles, a great necessity here, especially in
times of crisis, is not provided for. In the home country, a sick
wife will be nursed by the female relatives and not by the
husband. Husbands do not stay at home to look after children

or to do domestic jobs whilst the wives go out to work for short or long periods. Yet, following immigration, many newcomers will be faced with just such situations. Traditionally, the woman's place is at home and the husband's is outside; the latter's authority, however, both outside and within the home is indisputable. Motherhood and domesticity are the main roles in which a woman can experience a sense of achievement and satisfaction. The culture does not prepare the wife to take emergency or independent action in the face of crisis. Consequently, in the absence of the extended family here, the wife may be thrown very much on her own resources. If the husband dies or becomes incapacitated, the wife will be faced with the need to assume a great amount of responsibility and decision-making for which she has had no preparation by her culture. As a result, some immigrant wives go through considerable hardships. When in such a crisis they can be extremely dependent. Their dependency is again related to lack of cultural preparation for a more independent role, rather than to basic personality defect. Supportive help which aims at relieving them of some of the responsibilities and decision-making, should help these mothers to achieve a fair amount of self-dependence.

Though in the Indian, Pakistani, and, to some extent, Cypriot cultures, the husband is responsible for all external relationships and affairs of the family, the realities of life here are beginning to modify this. An increasing number of their women are now working or taking the children to clinics and schools, and going out shopping. The fact that all these activities were previously the concern of the father, may explain the great interest that these immigrant fathers retain in their children. They like to be consulted about them, and social workers should have less difficulty in involving them than they usually have with their English counterparts. In fact, it is doubtful whether a relationship or even contact can be established with any of these groups without the father's presence or very active support. A further point to be borne in mind is that Indian and Pakistani women, especially Moslems, avoid talking to or meeting men, or even women, from outside the family. Though they are generally very hospitable and take great pride in being visited, it would still be unwise to visit when the husband is not around. Cultural traditions will also determine what the family will discuss with an outsider, such as a social worker. The type of male-female roles assigned to members by the original culture will also affect what a man will discuss with a woman worker. The man's perception of a female worker differs considerably from that of a man accustomed to greater equality between the sexes. In this respect, there is a danger that social workers may react strongly to the submissive position of wives from these cultures. Serious difficulties can result if the worker encourages a wife either to talk about personal problems or to discuss family affairs in the absence of her husband. It is asking her to go against all her cultural and family traditions. Similarly, to encourage a lonely wife to take part in outside activities, without the husband's consent, or to try to foster more independence and assertiveness, could seriously hamper the relationship or upset the marital balance.

Most Asian women, especially Moslems, live very isolated and lonely lives here. Frequently they are frightened of going out alone, and their husbands keep them virtually in purdah. As they do not speak English, they are cut off from the local community. When their menfolk go out to work or their children go to school, they are left alone all day, 'a prey to loneliness and depression'. Of the many stories being told, there is one from Bradford about a distraught Pakistani woman whom the police found wandering about in the small hours of the morning. She had been here for eighteen months but was always confined to the house by her husband, until one night she could bear it no longer and went out for a walk when he was on shift work. She got lost and did not even know the name of her street or the number of her house. The relationship between male and female, especially among the Moslem immigrants, looked at by British cultural values, contains aspects of submission, degradation, and segregation, but alongside this the woman is offered the protection as well as the appreciation of her man. However, where a person is anxious to reject the claims and traditions of a husband or a parent or an original culture, as for example in a case of persistent gross cruelty, the social worker has a responsibility to respect such wishes and try to give intensive and long-term

support to enable the person to manage outside his traditional supportive agents.

There is some evidence that this pattern of relationship is
gradually changing, and no doubt the process and pressures
of immigration and the greater independence of working
wives here are bound to bring about a re-examination of the
husband–wife role in the light of these new influences. Some
redistribution of the present male superiority is bound to
follow, together with greater equity among the marital partners. Experience, however, from other immigrant groups suggests that this kind of reassignment is very gradual. It will
possibly affect the second or third generation of immigrants.
Some distinction should be made here about East African
Asians. Because of their identification with the British colonials in East Africa, this group of Asians took on a more British
middle-class style of life. Gradually caste has declined in
importance, women now eat at table with men, and there is
generally less rigidity of roles within the family. They still
hold onto many of their original customs such as arranged
marriages, but their pattern of life is more adapting and
evolving compared to immigrants from India and Pakistan.

Rightly or wrongly, immigrants—especially those from
India, Pakistan, and Cyprus—are very critical of British
society which they see as 'decadent' and 'immoral'. They are
very anxious about their children's outside contacts and are
often reluctant to let them associate with local young people.
For most of the children, the family will later decide whom
they are going to marry. In the case of Indian and Pakistani
children, some may already be betrothed to someone back
home. Child marriages are not uncommon in these two countries. The Probation Officer who suggests to a rather lonely
adolescent Indian boy that he join the local youth club,
quickly comes up against the family's strong resistance and its
fears about the possible effects of 'bad' influences on the boy.
They have a real anxiety, too, that he might meet a local girl
whom he will want to marry. The parents' anxieties are
raised so much sometimes that there have been instances of
girls being sent back to the home country to prevent their
associating with local boys. Illegitimacy among the Indians
and Pakistanis is rare, and this is not unconnected with the

severe family and cultural strictures. A pregnancy outside of marriage is the utmost disgrace. A bride's virginity is a matter of life or death especially in the villages. The woman and man who are discovered to have an illicit love relationship risk death by the men of the family. A child born out of wedlock is totally rejected.

Experience from work with immigrants shows that most immigrant children here are able to contain within themselves both their parents' standards and those of the outside community, without undue conflict and unhappiness. Where difficulties erupt, they usually point to other serious disturbances within the family or to lack of preparation for facing the greater rigours and strains of a complex society. For instance, most Moslem and Hindu girls live very sheltered lives and find it very difficult to cope with the greater demands and permissiveness of British life.

In contrast to these cultures, the traditional attitudes of West Indians to relationships between members of the opposite sex have been freer, with few taboos and restrictions. Prior to Emancipation, slaves were encouraged not to marry but to procreate, thus saving their plantation masters from the expense of having to buy new slaves from Africa. After Emancipation, common-law marriage by consent became the pattern. Extra-marital relationships are accepted as natural, and it is not at all uncommon for an unmarried girl to have children from more than one man. However, it is not socially acceptable to have them with someone who cannot maintain them. Marriage and family life are judged by how far they meet social standards and not on legitimacy. The increased identification, however, with the assumed values of the British middle classes, along with many West Indians' need to appear respectable and to be accepted, is making many mothers behave in a very strict and often punitive manner towards their adolescent daughters. Some West Indian girls rebel against what they feel to be unreasonable expectations, and a few become pregnant as a reaction to excessive control and stern sexual morality. The parents expect behaviour which contrasts greatly not only with their cultural background, but also with the values of the local working-class sub-culture with which they have more in common than with the middle-class ethos. The situation becomes even more explosive when the young girl has recently arrived from the West Indies and is suddenly expected to behave in ways contrasting greatly with her accustomed norms and standards. Irrespective of this, however, there is a greater probability that a child born out of wedlock to a West Indian mother will be accepted in his natural family than a child born to Indian or Pakistani mothers. This diverse outlook on illegitimacy is reflected also in plans about the child. Whereas most Indian and Pakistani mothers, under extreme pressure from their families, ask for the child to be placed for adoption, West Indian mothers generally prefer to keep them.

3. *Parent-child Interaction*

Among all immigrant groups children are generally much wanted and greatly loved. This love is usually demonstrated rather than expressed in words. In the Indian, Pakistani, and Cypriot cultures, boys are generally more valued than girls. The strongest tie among Indians is between father and son, and not between husband and wife. Children are mostly over-protected up to the age of five or six and then suddenly pushed towards too much, and too early, independence. They are expected to help in the fields and gradually to join the labour force at the earliest age. A kind of false early maturity and social competence is fostered which, under later stress, such as immigration, may show signs of regression. Because of the extended type of family life, parent-child interaction is less intense. Equally important to the child, and often as much influenced by them, are relatives and siblings; and this explains the strong ties that usually bind the wider kin.

Children may be scolded one moment and given to effusively the next. Physical punishment and verbal scolding are often used, but the former is more predominant among West Indian parents. Sending a child to his room or to bed early are not traditional forms of discipline, nor do parents see much point in them. As with affection and care, discipline is at times also tangibly demonstrated. The strict controls exercised by the family are reinforced by the community from outside. Such institutions as schools, religion, government, and the law are generally very authoritarian and directive. Good behaviour is externally inculcated rather than developed from within. The child avoids doing something mainly out of fear of being found out and shaming the family. The pattern of extended family group life favours the development of a kind of group ego and super ego which is mainly externally based, rather than developed from within. The kind of behaviour inculcated is that which facilitates group relationships, whilst certain kinds which are seen as detrimental are strongly disapproved. Because the individual's activities and life are mainly controlled from without, the inner world is not very well developed and this may explain why the process of self-examination is less meaningful with most immigrant clients than with local ones.

The greater permissiveness of the various institutions here throws both the adults and the children into some confusion. The permissive atmosphere of the English school, for example, is often found bewildering. Being used to severe punishments for minor misdemeanours, the immigrant child often fails to understand subtle reprimands; but if he is admonished more sternly he may also think the teacher is picking on him. Butterworth and Kinnisburgh[1] remark on how Indian and Pakistani children are at first very quiet, very respectful, and unduly deferential. In their attitude to education, the authors contrast them with West Indian children and quote the words of one education officer who said: 'The West Indian goes to school with a smack on his bottom, anxious to benefit from his education but not valuing it in itself. The Indian goes as he might go to church, to sit at the feet of his Guru.' Methods of working with these children will have to be adapted to take account of the earlier authoritarian influences that they have been exposed to. Children placed on probation or supervision, for instance, will need considerably more direction and control at first than do local children.

Indian, Pakistani, and Cypriot families with their home-centred cultures have a higher level of aspiration for their children, compared, for instance, with West Indian and English working-class families. West Indians, however, attach

[1] E. Butterworth and D. Kinnisburgh, *The Social Background of Immigrant Children from India, Pakistan and Cyprus* (London, Books for Schools, 1970).

great value to 'good behaviour' and condemn what they call rudeness. They sometimes exercise excessive control over their children and use very simple methods of punishment, including a fair number of beatings. In the absence of a stable male figure, discipline is usually enforced by the mother who acts both as mother and father to the growing child. In contrast to the patriarchal family system of the Indians, Pakistanis, and Cypriots, the West Indian family is more of a matriarchy. The West Indians' excessive zeal for good behaviour and absolute conformity often makes them appear cruel by local standards. The problem faced by many social workers here is to distinguish between a reasonable amount of discipline and what amounts to real cruelty by any cultural standards. In the face of what may appear to be cruelty and neglect, there is a real danger either of panicking and taking premature action, or of failing to protect the child by attributing this behaviour to cultural differences. The consistent and deep refusal of many West Indians to recognize that beatings do not help, can make a social worker feel helpless about how to handle the situation. There are instances when formal action is necessary to bring the reality of seriousness to the parents.

Amongst most of the immigrant groups there is no tradition of parents talking things over with their children. There is no sharing with them and they are not involved in decisions about themselves until late in life. This attitude can sometimes cause friction, but the parents' simple conviction that 'children do not understand anyway' can again paralyse any efforts at explaining a child's needs. A long educational process may have to follow. Young people in these cultures are not considered adult enough to be asked for their opinions or to share in decision-making until they marry, or, in the case of West Indians, until they have their own children. Yet, at the same time, the family and the culture say to young people, on the one hand, 'be seen and not heard', and, on the other, 'you are grown up now and you must earn your living and help us too'. The extended family fosters a prolonged type of dependency, possibly because it needs the full support of all its members for survival. For similar reasons, parents do not recognize adolescent rebellion or the need of the growing-up child to be a separate person. In fact, they see adolescent revolt as being a very abnormal form of behaviour. The explanation for this may be two-fold: (a) Adolescent revolt, as we know it here, is mainly an attempt by the growing adolescent to establish his individual identity in a society where great stress is placed on the individual and on self-dependence. In societies like the ones already described, where the stress is on the family group, we can talk less of an individual identity and more of a collective one. The fate of the growing adolescent is bound up with and dependent on that of all the others within the group. (b) Unlike Western societies, where there is less interaction between child and adult outside family situations, in the peasant areas from where most immigrants come, the prevailing pattern is quite different. The child from very early on, moves in a world of adults, works side by side with them, and shares many of their experiences. There is no clear demarcation between childhood and adulthood though, as mentioned earlier, this does not stop the older people from not recognizing adulthood in the young person until his marriage. By this time, the young married man is anxious to contribute to the success of his group, and group rather than individual considerations prevail.

The process of immigration, establishment of a more nuclear type of family here, the greater stress on individualism, and the pressures of a youth culture are fostering a need for individual identity in young blacks and this is beginning to bring some of them into conflict with their parents. The parents, influenced by their own cultural experiences, want to perpetuate a type of group loyalty and family group identity. This, however, is meaningless to the child who is brought up in a nuclear type of family and in a society bearing no resemblance to the parents' original culture. The strength of the parental and cultural control, as well as the reaction to it, is illustrated in the following example: An Indian girl of sixteen threatened to kill herself by jumping from the window if her parents insisted on her arranged betrothal. The mother equally felt that the girl was better dead than disobedient. Social workers working with immigrant adolescents should avoid the danger of identifying with the child against the authoritarian parents. Such an identification is likely to increase the parents' defensiveness and the child's anxiety. Any help given to the adolescent must be given within the context of his family and not in opposition to it, unless there are very important reasons why the adolescent should be supported to manage, perhaps temporarily, outside his family. This might be considered, for instance, in the case of an adolescent Hindu girl whose life is threatened by the family because she is expecting an illegitimate child.

4. *The Expression and Significance of Feeling and Communication*

In the social work process, language assumes great importance as a means of communicating ideas, feelings, and attitudes. Where social worker and client lack a common language, the possibilities for misunderstanding are infinite. The introduction of an interpreter is not a satisfactory solution as it introduces a third element that complicates the relationship. It would obviously be more satisfactory if the social worker, black or white, could speak the immigrant's respective language. However, the employment of social workers from the same background as the respective immigrant group can give rise to many difficulties unless it is based on a well thought out programme.

Next to language, feeling and the way it is handled is perhaps the most meaningful form of human communication. Unawareness of how people from unfamiliar backgrounds deal with their feelings can lead to miscommunication and inaccurate assessments. An inappropriate assessment of feeling can jeopardize the outcome of social work contact. The way people from different backgrounds express such feelings as grief, pain, anger, and joy can differ considerably. Real personal communication between the worker and the client will depend on an accurate evaluation of the strength and meaning of the latter's attitudes and real feelings.

Immigrants from the West Indies and Cyprus, for instance, tend to express their moods, feelings, and desires more readily and more demonstratively than British people. It has been noticed, too, that children from these backgrounds fly into tempers more easily than local ones, but the anger also subsides quickly. Though in both these cultures authoritarian institutions, as well as the family, often exercise repressive controls, these do not extend to the expression of emotions. The family and the community display and approve the expression of strong group and personal emotions. Among the Cypriots the display of one's moods and desires appears to be more important than personal success. The behaviour of such immigrants as West Indians and Cypriots may appear more belligerent than it is intended to be, because feelings for them are real only when they are clearly and spontaneously expressed. The uninhibited and volatile expression of such feeling can be felt as very threatening by local people and by social workers unused to it.

These groups are used to experiencing and demonstrating feeling rather than talking or writing about it. In these circumstances it would be rather futile for social workers to try to encourage them to verbalize feelings. The intense anger or depression of a West Indian may appear overwhelming and frightening and could easily inhibit a social worker who might try to withdraw from the situation. A West Indian couple who visited their daughter in a Children's Home started shouting abuse at the staff for allegedly being unkind to their daughter. Very hostile threats were uttered in the process. The staff were naturally frightened and at a loss as to how to handle them. As the man went on and on shouting, the wife suddenly asked him 'to be quiet and shut up'. They calmed down and on leaving the Home they turned round and shouted to everybody, 'good night, love'. Because of the comparative lack of inhibitions and controls, both positive and negative feelings may take extreme forms. Thus, the gloom of a West Indian's depression, although quite alarming, if judged by British standards, is appropriate by those of West Indians. The recovery from such depression can be spontaneous. Joy and pleasure equally take a more exuberant form when judged by local standards. With some West Indians, especially women, chronic depression and apathy are not infrequent. This is usually brought about by feelings of homesickness, the effects of an unwelcoming climate, serious housing difficulties, and lack of environmental stimulation, as well as the pressure to hold down a full-time job. (The effects of such depression on the children of immigrants is well described by Dr. Stewart-Prince in a later paper in this book.)

A reassuring observation arising from work with such families is that they respond well to support which does not make many demands on them. The way to reach them, however, is to go out to them rather than to expect them to turn up at agencies. Not only is there no cultural tradition of keeping regular appointments at agencies, but also the depressive element seriously affects their capacity for any extra effort. Arrangements for play-centres, or nurseries, or short holidays for the children, help to alleviate the mother's pressures and make her task appear more manageable.

In contrast to the Cypriots and West Indians, Pakistanis and Indians are more inhibited in their expression of emotions. Relationships within the family are more formal and there is a considerable amount of repression of intimate feelings. There is considerable taboo also on the display of public emotion, especially by women, except on someone's death. The extreme politeness of Indians, which mainly arises from a strong denial of negative feelings, can create as great a feeling of impotence in the social worker as the belligerence of Cypriots or the volatile behaviour of West Indians. In the same way that Indians tend to deny their aggressive feelings, they also fail to recognize negative feelings in others and try to convince themselves that everything is all right. The tendency also to reassure others that everything will be all right possibly arises from their wish not to make demands on others and to avoid giving the impression of being in need; the latter is seen as involving 'a loss of face'. Cypriots, too, tend to over-promise, mainly because they do not like to upset or disappoint the other person, which possibly indicates their low capacity for tolerating pain in themselves and others. In either case, it is difficult to establish a working relationship unless their underlying denials or fears are understood and appropriately challenged.

5. *The Concept of Time and Events*

In the cultures from which most immigrants come, time and punctuality have not yet acquired the value ascribed to them by industrial societies. For most immigrants time is 'how you feel'. They live more in the present, and though orientated towards the future, they are also afraid of it. As a result, they try to control it by interpreting many situations and signs in terms of future happenings. They have no tradition of making appointments in advance or of arranging beforehand to visit relatives and friends. People just drop in and expect to be seen or entertained. It is little use trying to offer them appointments at the beginning of contact. Time has to be made for them when they happen to come, which can be a day or two after the agreed appointment. Similarly, they do not expect the worker to arrange visits in advance. Too much advance arrangement is seen as formality and impedes real contact. Many house-parents and foster-parents, unfamiliar with this attitude, have been annoyed when West Indians or Cypriots have suddenly turned up to visit a child. Also, the tendency of West Indians to visit in groups of five or six has often generated considerable discomfort and sometimes even ill-feeling.

Immigrants are also unaccustomed to celebrating birthdays and wedding anniversaries and to exchanging presents on such occasions. The pattern of writing letters to children is also unfamiliar because back home they rarely had a child away and the need to write never arose. There is also the feeling that 'children do not mind' or 'they do not understand'. House-mothers and foster-parents, again, are often critical of immigrant parents for failing to send birthday or Christmas cards, or presents, or to write frequently to their children.

The Adaptation of Methods

A different emphasis may have to be given to certain social work methods in order to take account of the way immigrants experience and express their feelings and of the assignments of roles within the family, as well as of the impact of very authoritarian institutions in their lives. In work with immigrants, social workers may have to choose to be more demonstrative and more active and directive than they are accustomed to be with many of their local clients. They will be expected to put things over more explicitly, and less subtly and vaguely. Passivity and too many efforts to try to help immigrant clients to 'reach their own solutions', are likely to be interpreted as inadequate response and lack of interest. Similarly, methods aimed at promoting self-examination and self-awareness are only rarely appropriate. Such methods run the danger of increasing the distance between the worker's perception of his function and the client's expectation of the contact. Stressing, for instance, self-responsibility and independence to people who have been accustomed to extended interdependent relationships, can amount to a form of neglect. Again, in many instances reality needs to be stressed clearly and unmistakably. It is obviously necessary for the worker to avoid appearing as the white boss who always knows what is best, thus arousing memories of colonial rule.

Immigrants do not distinguish social workers from other 'officials' carrying authority. In the home country, even minor officials are seen as very powerful people who must not be upset, even though they are generally held in low opinion because of their misuse of authority. The social worker is vulnerable to these same attitudes—which also explains why many immigrants appear inhibited when in touch with authority figures here.

Touch, as a form of communication, is most meaningful to most immigrants and in fact with some a relationship cannot be established without shaking hands or touching the shoulder or hand at an appropriate moment. The response from a spontaneous action of this kind can be remarkable, provided that touch is not used as a gimmick. This way of working may not come easily to social workers who are unused to demonstrating interest more actively or to assuming a more directive role within the social work relationship. After all, local social workers will themselves have been differently influenced and shaped by their own culture in which interest and concern are sincerely meant but not expressed. The following illustrative comment was made by an Indian after a number of interviews with his social worker: 'She very nice lady but not say much.'

Interviews with immigrant clients facing problems of interpersonal relationships can be spaced further apart than such meetings with local clients. This is mainly because the discussion of personal difficulties usually necessitates a fair amount of introspection, self-examination, and verbalizing of feeling. For reasons stated earlier on, immigrants are unused to such processes. Occasional interviews with them have the same intensity and implications as more frequent ones with local people. Insistence on too many visits will generate both anxiety and hostility—and the latter is unlikely to be directly expressed.

Many immigrants show a capacity for a deep denial of very obvious things and situations, which by local standards can be interpreted as psychotic behaviour. This is not, however, a type of behaviour which is put up to protect precarious defences, and it can be challenged without fear that the client will break down. Social work with immigrants has also demonstrated that it is more meaningful, at the beginning stages especially, to work predominantly on the 'here and now', rather than on the 'here and then'. The 'here and now' makes sense to them because there are many current reality difficulties on which to concentrate. The difficulties of many immigrants are predominantly reactions to stress and conflicts from current life situations rather than psychopathological, though the latter is not excluded. Also, past personal experiences are not usually shared within the family, and, therefore, not retained to be reproduced and related to current behaviour. It is mostly the present, as well as current behaviour and happenings, that is real and meaningful to most immigrants. For these reasons and also because of the way they experience and perceive time, it is almost impossible, not to say futile, to try to obtain a developmental history.

Some of the methods outlined above have also been found to be equally appropriate for local clients who have been described as 'infantile' or 'immature' or who can only respond to such methods because of their special sub-cultural experiences. In the case of immigrants, the need for the use of these methods is based on a differential diagnosis related to specific cultural experiences and to current stresses arising from the effects of immigration and often discrimination rather than to major personality defects. It is for similar reasons that it is also dangerous to equate immigrants with the more underprivileged clients of the local community.

Conclusion

A full understanding of clients' situations cannot be reached without taking notice of their cultural and sub-cultural experiences. Immigrants bring with them the reality world of their cultural group as well as their methods of coping. An emotional grasp of the immigrants' reality world and of their cultural values, traditions, and habitual forms of behaviour, enables the social worker to separate cultural from pathological behaviour and, especially, to use his skills and his methods to suit the clients' needs.

Some groups of immigrants are better able to contain their difficulties than others and this largely depends on the organization and cohesion of the family group. Not all the problems faced by immigrants are material ones or problems of coping with new situations. The outward overlay of material needs may conceal considerable personality difficulties and family dysfunctioning. Experience, however, suggests that new immigrants are more accessible to measures intended to alleviate pressing social needs than problems of interpersonal relationships. In social work with immigrant groups, the basic principles and methods of the social work profession apply, but certain modifications may be necessary to take account of culturally determined differences and of current stresses and conflicts. Social workers may have to be prepared to accept far more dependency initially than they are accustomed to, to use more directive methods, to be far more explicit, to demonstrate greater interest, and to concentrate more on the 'here and now' and on real current anxieties. Methods aimed at furthering self-awareness or too much self-direction are likely to meet with less success.

II | The Social Worker's Cultural Pattern as it Affects Casework with Immigrants

Bessie Kent[1]

Culture may be defined as 'the complex whole that includes knowledge, belief, art, morals, law, customs and any other capabilities and habits acquired by man as a member of society'.[2] We are ourselves carriers of our culture as the immigrant is a carrier of his, and it is therefore necessary, in order to understand the interaction between ourselves and immigrants, to look at the ways in which the individual's cultural pattern is integrated into his personality structure, the particular cultural patterns of the social worker and the immigrant, and the implications which the resultant conflict has for social casework, assuming that where two separate cultures meet, conflict is inevitable.

Cultural Pattern and Personality Formation

Social custom affects the child long before he is born. The place of birth, means of birth, ante-natal care—even, one could say, the moment of conception—are to some extent culturally determined. From birth onwards, heavy cultural pressures bear on the child and those who are responsible for him. The child experiences the unique feeling which his parents have for him, of which psycho-analytic theory has made us very aware, but he also experiences through his parents the limitations on behaviour and the expectations of the society in which he lives. In turn, he interprets these demands, so that the child grows up with a culture composed of what

[1] This paper has been reprinted from *Social Work* (Vol. 22, No. 4, October 1965).

Bessie Kent is Principal Lecturer in Social Work at Leeds Polytechnic.

[2] Gardner Murphy, quoted by S. W. Ginsburg in 'The Impact of the Social Worker's Cultural Structure on Social Therapy', *Social Casework* (Vol. 32, No. 8, October 1951), p. 319.

others about him think the cultural pattern is plus what he makes of their interpretation.[1] These demands, which constitute a form of social control, are internalized; they are integrated as part of the ego and superego and remain an operative part of the unconscious personality. Children want to identify not only with their parents but with their parents' ideals and standards, and the net effect of this process is to bring about socially acceptable behaviour on the part of the child.[2]

As the standards become internalized, they form an enduring inner self-control system. Even in later years, the process of identification and internalization continues. It would seem that the formal controls, expressed in legal sanctions, are generally less effective in modifying behavior; such sanction appears to be less powerful in producing long-term positive results.[3]

It is this concept of the internalization of cultural patterning which is of particular importance in considering problems of acculturation—that is, the modification of the immigrants' original pattern. While it is true that such patterns are modifiable, I would like to suggest that an analogy can be found in intra-psychic development, in that while we expect marriage to be an adaptive experience, the primitive mother-child relationship is a very strong determinant of the adaptation made. In other words, while very considerable cultural adaptations can be made, that cultural adaptation incorporated earliest in life will continue as a basic personality factor and will be regressed to in times of stress. This means that we cannot ever think in terms of complete acculturation.

Another important factor to recognize is that the ability to adapt to new cultural demands is directly related to the degree of maturity of the personality of the individual. It is the mature, secure person who finds change and growth easiest; insecurities and feelings of inadequacy strengthen regressive cultural tendencies. These factors apply to ourselves

[1] W. V. Gioseffi, 'Culture as an Aspect of Total Personality', *Social Casework* (Vol. 40, No. 3, March 1959), p. 115.

[2] I. Weisman and J. Chwast, 'Control and Values in Social Work Treatment', in *Social Casework in the Fifties* (New York, F.S.S.A., 1962), p. 253.

[3] Ibid., pp. 256-7.

as well as to immigrants; the more uncertain we are, the more British we become.

It is because culture is internalized that social change and adaptation are often strongly resisted. Cultural adaptations may involve not only intra-psychic defences but also actions or beliefs which may never have been permitted before and which are, therefore, unacceptable. Values which have been internalized cannot easily be rejected and demands to change against one's value system will occasion considerable anxiety.[1]

We need, however, to be cautious about making generalizations about cultural resistance to change. The resistance is sometimes occasioned not from unconscious or conscious reluctance but because the demands of the new cultural pattern have been inadequately conveyed; there may have developed a conflict between the person's internal striving and his effective carrying-out of role.[2] If he does not know what is expected of him, he cannot do it—even if he wants to! Where difficulties lie here, the social worker's function will be educative; where at subconscious level there is intercultural conflict between the social worker and the client, further analysis of the problem will be necessary. We will be quick to look at the immigrant's cultural pattern as a possible cause of the difficulty; we will be less speedy to examine our own. Since, in Britain, social workers have for the most part been drawn from the middle class, it is important to consider the cultural patterns which have contributed to the shaping of these social workers.

The British Middle-class Cultural Pattern

A Greek LL.D. recently commented: 'The salient feature of the British middle class is its lack of a salient feature.' It has been interesting to note how difficult it has been for both British and non-British to assess the outstanding characteristics of middle-class behaviour, the goals and aspirations, the circumscriptions. This in itself makes life difficult for aliens; there is an assumption that the rules of the game are known and failure to abide by them is an indication of bad taste.

[1] Gioseffi, pp. 116–17.

[2] H. H. Perlman, *Social Casework: A Problem-Solving Process* (Chicago, University of Chicago Press, 1957), p. 24.

Where the rules are not clear even to the local white community, how is the immigrant to discover them?

The British passion for privacy and the well-known reserve account for part of the difficulty in assessing middle-class cultural patterns, which have so far remained almost completely unstudied due, I presume, to difficulties in obtaining information about what would seem to the British to be extremely personal matters. There are, however, some outstanding characteristics which are of importance in casework with immigrants.

'In Great Britain odd and eccentric behaviour in persons in the community is more easily tolerated.'[1] There is, perhaps, no great insistence on conformity and this might allow for diversity of behaviour in immigrants. Does this tolerance extend to others? A look at British insularity and its dogmatic assertion of rightness tends to indicate that the supposed tolerance may amount more to a self-assured righteousness which, when involved with foreigners, becomes omniscient indifference. A British business man, who had stayed at a Norwegian hotel at the head of a fjord—at which the hotel manager's wife was a Scot and the waitress Irish—commented when asked if he had any language difficulty, 'Oh, no, there weren't any foreigners there'. A British surgeon refused to enter the *Étrangers* queue at Marseilles customs on the grounds that he wasn't a foreigner!

It is not so much that the foreigner is tolerated, it is more that he is not noted. The implication of this for work with aliens is obvious. As an indication that this may be true, I would point to the figures recently published in the 1961 Census.[2] Of a population of roughly 46 million persons, $2\frac{1}{2}$ million (if one includes persons born in the Republic of Ireland) are not native-born. Even allowing for the fact that some persons born outside England and Wales will have been reared in the middle-class pattern (e.g. children of British colonials), one can safely say that by 1961 one person in every twenty-three came from a foreign cultural pattern.

If one can assume that social work journals reflect accurately

---

[1] Margit Tornudd, *Case Conference* (Vol. 4, No. 9, March 1958).
[2] General Register Office, *1961 Census: England and Wales, Birthplace and Nationality Tables* (London, H.M.S.O., 1964).

areas of interest of social workers, English social workers, too, remained indifferent to the foreigners on their shores. Looking back through *Social Work, Case Conference, The Almoner,* and the *British Journal of Psychiatric Social Work* from 1947 to 1961, one finds three articles only which are even remotely concerned with casework with immigrants; there is no mention of the 750,000 people born outside the Commonwealth but resident in Britain and no real awareness of the problems of acculturation.

From 1958 to 1962, in a community which had had no noticeable influx of immigrants and was completely unaware of having any non-native population, seven out of the sixty children with whom I was involved at the Child Guidance Clinic had one or both parents who were non-native whites; in other words, over 10 per cent of the families had immigrant connections. This may not have been a representative sample but it does indicate that during this time many caseworkers were dealing with many immigrants without a conscious awareness of the immigrant identity. Long before the national interest in immigrants became vocal, problems of inter-cultural conflict existed in British social work but remained unrecognized. In ignoring this problem, social workers have reflected the British middle-class pattern.

Another major area of difficulty in working with immigrants occasioned by the cultural pattern is that of the taboo on the free expression of feeling. Whatever is responsible for the British reserve, the effect is to produce a cultural barrier between the British and those whose patterns are more permissive. Our casework concept of 'the free expression of feeling' suffers severe cultural limitations! A South American teacher of social work was recently astonished to find that one of our major problems in teaching is to get students to bring out their feelings; her experience was exactly contrary, since her students, including the males, laugh, cry, exude aggression to such an extent that she has difficulty in getting them to be quiet long enough to make any intellectual progress. In a paper presented to the Association of Psychiatric Social Workers, Mr. Triseliotis[1] gave an instance of the way in

---

[1] J. Triseliotis, 'Cultural Factors and Casework Implications', *British Journal of Psychiatric Social Work* (Vol. VIII, No. 1, 1965), pp. 15–25.

which his English colleagues were alarmed in overhearing and misinterpreting a violent, noisy interview between himself and a Cypriot woman.

The taboo on the free expression of feeling is very extensive within the English cultural pattern and pervades many areas of life; Ivy Compton-Burnett and Benjamin Britten have a brilliance of intellect, an originality that is always fascinating, but at the same time, there is a remoteness, a detachment, a lack of involvement which is typically British. It is not accidental that an outstanding English social work theorist defines casework without mentioning the client as a human being,[1] and speaks of clients engaging themselves with policy or method[2]—not the human embodiment of that policy and method in the form of the caseworker!

British middle-class patterns will also alienate the social worker from the immigrant. Immigrants will often find themselves with families structured much more similarly to those of the British working class than the middle class. Working-class and immigrant families will tend to be composed of couples in close-knit social networks, where husbands and wives are expected to have a rigid division of labour, with little stress on the importance of shared interests and joint recreation. It is expected that wives would have many relationships with their relatives, and husbands with their friends. Both partners can get help from people outside the family which makes the rigid division of labour between husband and wife possible. Successful sexual relations are not considered essential to a happy marriage. In contrast, families in loose networks (as in the middle class) have a less rigid division of labour, stress the importance of shared interests and joint recreation, and place a good deal of emphasis on the importance of successful sexual relations.[3] A British social worker confronted with a Pole who felt he had fulfilled his marital role by providing a house and food for his wife, might easily be tempted to open up to him the glories of a middle-

---

[1] N. Timms, *Social Casework: Principles and Practice* (London, Routledge & Kegan Paul, 1964), p. 7.

[2] Ibid., p. 10.

[3] Elizabeth Bott, *Family and Social Network* (London, Tavistock Publications, 1957), p. 198.

class marital relationship with all its stress on shared pleasures and responsibilities, thus alienating her client from herself!

More than any other national group, the British seem to have had the greatest difficulty in finding pleasure in their children. The pattern of sending children away from home at a very early age extends back into the Middle Ages, and foreigners visiting England in the fifteenth century considered this practice the mark of barbarism. While our attitudes about children are in the process of changing, I suggest that this dis-ease with children is a particular barrier between us and those to whom the indulgence of childhood is an essential part of the cultural pattern. Where dependency needs are openly accepted, the need for guidance is strong, but so also is the pleasure in the dependency of children.

A young West African, with a considerable criminal record in this country, used to stay with my husband and myself quite frequently in between prison sentences. It eventually became clear that my husband had to act as an external superego, being willing, at any time of the day or night, to give firm instructions about how to behave in moments of crisis. Eventually, the superego became internalized and the man seems able to survive on his own without further trouble. However, at the time that he was unable to manage this, the remarkable thing was that, hard-working as he was, he had unlimited time for children, and his moments of greatest pleasure seemed to be the hours he would spend contemplating the young children, occasionally being active, but for the most part passively enjoying their childhood. It was an exquisite pleasure to him merely to watch them. I have never known an English or American father who would not have had to be 'doing' something with the child. How difficult it is for us to accept and appreciate this passivity.

In summary, the middle-class traits which seem most to contribute to inter-cultural conflict in social work are the reserve in personal relationships, insularity, the pattern of family relationships, and the intolerance of dependence. Paradoxically, there is also some tolerance of diversity in others and a long-standing tradition of justice which will at least mean an attempt to see that the immigrant receives fair treatment.

Casework as a Sub-culture

Casework as we know it developed in England, was exported through the Charity Organisation Society to the United States, was then elaborated and conceptualized there and, in turn, exported back to Britain. In time, the differences between British and American casework, largely determined by their respective cultures, will become clarified, but for the time being there is enough similarity so that we may consider for both countries casework as a sub-cultural development.

Caseworkers are themselves involved, to some extent, in inter-cultural conflict. Bred within a culture which has little tolerance for social failure, they assert the worth of the individual, regardless of his accomplishments, and in their professional activities have formed a culture within a culture.[1] Similarly, the encouragement of the outward expression of emotion is in conflict with the pattern recognized by the social worker's larger cultural group. None the less, casework could only have developed within the context of a Protestant, democratic society, and the fundamental assumptions of casework, as noted by Florence Hollis, are also the fundamental assumptions of our society,[2] so that the deviations we are prepared to tolerate (or even to see) will be severely limited by our cultural patterning.

An American supervisor had a Chinese post-graduate student who was in her second-year field placement. For the first five months of this placement, the student was completely unable to recognize any form of hostile feeling; despite intelligence and an English-speaking education from the age of twelve, she was, as a result of the Chinese insistence on politeness and reverence, blind to all expressions of anger and resentment. At the time, this blindness seemed remarkable; this was in the days before social work became 'culture conscious'. Today, we would consider even more remarkable the fact that it took a highly intelligent, skilled, and sensitive supervisor at least three months to recognize the source of the

---

[1] O. Pollak, 'Cultural Dynamics in Casework', in C. Kasius (ed.), *Social Casework in the Fifties* (New York, F.S.S.A., 1962), p. 89.

[2] F. Hollis, 'Principles and Assumptions Underlying Casework Practice', Appendix II, in J. Heywood, *An Introduction to Casework Skills* (London, Routledge & Kegan Paul, 1964), pp. 160–2.

difficulty, since her social worker's sub-culture, as well as her more general pattern, assumed the existence of anger as a natural feeling and in turn blinded her to the inter-cultural conflict which was the basis of the difficulty. Since we tend to assume the rightness of our own patterns of behaviour and thought, we are often oblivious to their existence.

Dr. Ginsburg asserts that the social worker's choice of vocation is heavily influenced by cultural patterning.

Although, as far as I know, no accurate data have been compiled on the factors determining the choice of social work as a profession, it is fair to assume, I think, that such a choice must, most often, represent a need to help people in a profession that enjoys considerable prestige and allows one to exercise a degree of power over the lives of others. Such factors must clearly influence the worker's attitudes towards his clients. It may be fairly stated that consciously or otherwise we help people to be like ourselves.[1]

It has been my experience both here and in the United States—working in clinics where clients came from all social and income groups—that the middle-class social worker may find the middle-class client stimulating and challenging, but that there is seldom the relaxed ease in working with them which we find with people from backgrounds different from ours. There may be a variety of reasons for this, but I would suggest that a major factor is that, consciously or unconsciously, we choose to work with weak, inadequate people in order to satisfy our own needs for the security which comes from feeling more competent than others. Writing about two social workers whom he had analysed, Dr. Ginsburg says: 'Their own attitudes materially affected their relationships with clients and resulted in such overcompensatory, overprotective attitudes towards them as to influence their work seriously.'[2]

Another way of saying much the same thing is: social work as a sub-culture permits the expression and use of aggression and authority for people who feel guilty about the 'power complex' of their major cultural grouping; we social workers have to gain our power subtly, through having other people

---

[1] Ginsburg, p. 321.
[2] Ibid., p. 324.

dependent on us. The early caseworkers seemed heartless in their expectations that all people could live up to middle-class standards; we are perhaps in danger of the opposite error, in that through our feelings of superiority we may demand too little. This is of particular relevance in our work with immigrants. 'It may very well be that some of the white workers are less demanding of high standards of compliance and achievement in their Negro clients because of their [the workers'] culturally imposed estimate of the Negroes' capacities and potentialities.'[1]

Paradoxically, it may be necessary for us to alter our basic ideas about the need for self-determination when dealing with people from cultural backgrounds which differ from ours since their needs may mean our acceptance of their dependence on us. This is a difficult thing to do, not only because our cultural pattern insists on independence of action but also because our pattern is perhaps more protective of us as social workers; if the responsibility for decision and action lies with the client and failure results, it is easier for us to absolve ourselves from blame. In this way, some casework with immigrants challenges us to take a responsibility which we may fear. We like to have people dependent on us but not so obviously so that their failure appears to be a result of our bad judgment.

Inter-cultural Problems in Casework with Immigrants

The problem of casework with immigrants is primarily a problem of conflicting values; only in this respect does it differ from the more usual forms of casework and even then it bears many similarities to the more familiar problems of casework with others who do not share the dominant cultural pattern. If we think of casework with immigrants as comparable to casework with delinquents or the mentally ill or the East End working class, we may be able to get some perspective on the problem and will no longer need to isolate the immigrant so completely in our thinking.

Many social workers are now aware of the problems for immigrants in conforming to the expectations of the British

[1] Ibid., p. 322.

cultural pattern; what we must also be conscious of is the knowledge that because our own cultural patterns were ingrained so early and at such depth in our personalities, intimate contact with persons from different cultures is bound to challenge our standards and set up unconscious antagonisms. Because certain ways of behaving and thinking are important to us we want to convince others of their value. For instance, we are convinced that we can do something about our fate, that man can take responsibility for his destiny. Many immigrants come from cultural patterns which would view such ideas as more than folly. Man is seen as a helpless being whose role in life is to accept without complaint the futility of life. The potential clash here is great indeed: the client who will not 'move' and the goading social worker!

So long as one remains at a distance, the idea of cultural relativity, of tolerating the conflicting expectations and reaction patterns, of thinking, 'Although it's not for me, it may be right for him', makes a possible *modus vivendi*; when closeness is established, the proposition that one way of living may be as successful as another encounters a great deal of resistance. Because our cultural pattern is a basic component of our unconscious personality, 'to accept emotionally all the implications of cultural relativity would mean, in the last analysis, to deny one's superego and one's ego structure'.[1]

The areas of greatest threat for the social worker in work with immigrants are problems of aggressiveness and sexuality, but there may also be difficulties when the worker is confronted with different standards of family living, hygiene and appearance, attitudes towards property and privacy, and vocational aspirations.[2]

When working with immigrants, even if we maintain a degree of objectivity while at the same time becoming involved in an intimate relationship—a more difficult casework task than usual because of the inter-cultural conflict—we none the less have to face the problem of whether we do, in fact, *have* to impose some of our values and controls on our immigrant clients. This would seem to me to be a most difficult problem for caseworkers in their work with clients from a

[1] Pollak, p. 87.
[2] Weisman and Chwast, p. 260.

different cultural background. Can acculturation be forced? Should it be forced? What is the role of the caseworker in either instance?

The easiest approach to this problem is to rule out one situation where there is no problem! Where the client's social difficulty is related to inter-cultural conflict solely because he has insufficient knowledge of our culture's expectations, the social worker has a simple educative function. By furnishing the necessary knowledge, he should enable the client to solve his own problem. With immigrants we can be of particular use as a teacher of role, but to do this 'the caseworker must himself be clear as to what, realistically, the role's requirements are, its firm requisites, and the range of variation permissible within it'.[1] As indicated earlier, there has been insufficient study of our culture and its role requirements, and caseworkers cannot, therefore, be clear about this. In this respect, we are lacking in the tools necessary for our trade.

The difficulty in casework with immigrants arises when there is a clash in values. We dislike seeing ourselves as agents of social control, but it is essentially true that 'social work treatment . . . is one of society's alternative ways of exercising social control of persons who manifest deviant behavior'.[2] The acceptance of this control function means that we are prepared to represent the norms and standards which are basic to our society. Acknowledging the need for flexibility, we are nevertheless confronted with the need to select those values which are essential to social functioning and to look at the implications of our control function as it affects casework with immigrants.

As with other problems of social control in casework, we are seldom able to force the acceptance of our values—even if we want to do so. Ours is, rather, the responsibility of helping reveal the inter-cultural conflict and, through offering a pattern of identification, enabling the client to resolve it.

This calls for the caseworker's appreciation not only of the conflict that exists between the various cultural values but also of the significance of the pressures exerted by the respective cultures to

[1] Perlman, p. 25.
[2] Weisman and Chwast, p. 252.

make the individual conform. The risk of the worker's being unwittingly one of these pressures needs recognition.[1]

It has been argued that the social worker needs to play a more active part in hastening the process of acculturation, and that:

treatment goals must take into account the extent to which the surrounding culture will permit the client to go, but go he must, if he is to benefit from casework help. Without some loosening of the grip his culture has had on him, change and movement are likely to be impossible.[2]

Perhaps the answer is that while we must make clear the minimal standards of value and behaviour which our society will tolerate, the immigrant client must choose for himself the most comfortable mode of accommodating himself to our demands.

What are the implications for the casework process of these problems of inter-cultural values? I referred earlier to the process of unconscious identification as the mechanism by which the cultural pattern is incorporated into the personality structure, and noted that this is an ongoing process. As with most casework, a major factor in change is enabling the client to identify with the social worker, but, as with all our clients, the immigrant is unable to identify with that which is completely foreign to him.

If we expect him to develop inner controls, the values cannot be alien to him. We know, psychodynamically, that social approval is an important factor in the incorporation of values. Social approval includes the worker's approval, which can be a powerful dynamic when experienced by the client. . . . This kind of value focus and its implementation in the treatment process may provide the worker with a foundation for helping clients build healthy internal controls. Such controls, when based on both the client's values and the values implicit in our own social structure, permit a real expression of an individual's potentialities in our democratic society.[3]

[1] W. V. Gioseffi, 'The Relationship of Culture to the Principles of Casework', *Social Casework* (Vol. 32, No. 5, May 1951), pp. 190–6.
[2] Pollak, p. 92.
[3] Weisman and Chwast, p. 260.

There are, after all, basic approaches to social living; if we can help the client to see what we have in common, he may be better able to accept what is different. In this, the social worker needs to be imaginative.

Casework treatment is complicated by inter-cultural conflict since such conflict detracts from the capacity to change. Because cultural patterns are internalized, demands for change threaten the personality structure, thus increasing resistance to change. 'Even if one has perchance rejected his group and its outward mores, he cannot as easily reject the values that are internalized and have become enduring patterns with which he guards his security.'[1] Realizing this, the social worker must initially permit the client to maintain his cultural identity, helping him to find other means of satisfaction before he can be expected to consider modifying the values learned in another cultural setting. This may to some extent be accomplished by careful selection of areas where the social worker can offer the client social approval, but he must select these areas not on the basis of what is of value in his culture but, rather, on the basis of what is of value in the immigrant's culture which is also acceptable within his own culture.

In other words, the help we offer is the product of our own general knowledge of personality and social conditions, of our understanding of this individual and his situation, and our value system. The help the client uses must be consistent with his own vision for himself.[2]

Acculturation through identification must begin within the limits of the client's own culture and if in our anxiety to make him like ourselves we try to force the pace, we shall again only intensify the resistances. One can encourage an Englishwoman to solve her problems by developing outside interests; this solution is not available to a Pakistani woman.

Work with immigrants presents some specific diagnostic problems. The caseworker is often confronted not only with difficulties of communication but with diagnostic uncertainty; ignoring cultural patterns may mean assuming the existence

[1] Gioseffi, 'Culture as an Aspect of the Total Personality', p. 115
[2] Hollis, p. 157.

of deviation or illness which does not in fact exist. On the other hand, problems of inter-cultural conflict can in themselves cause personality deterioration. Miss J. Cottle, Senior Psychiatric Social Worker, Bradford Mental Health Service, has furnished an example of these diagnostic perplexities:

A twelve-year-old Indian boy, who had what appeared to us to be a deeply rooted phobic state, was referred to the Child Guidance Clinic. Since the death of a small brother five years previously, he had been complaining of fears of dying, of feeling faint, of palpitations. He was unable to go to school in case he died whilst he was there; in recent weeks he had not been able to stay at his parents' house for the same reason and had been staying near by with an uncle. The mother was never seen despite all efforts—originally the uncle and father came and then the father only.

The onset of the illness was discussed with him in Western terms of trauma at the death of the younger brother and possible ambivalence to him before his death. The father looked blank and said that this could not possibly be so as about half the children had died in the family and this was the normal pattern of Indian family life—the British pattern of child survival seemed very strange to him!

At the next interview, the reason for the child's apparent sudden dislike of the parental home was explored; it was quite clear to the father that it was the house and not the family which was the trouble, since the boy became unable to stay in the house a few months after removal from a small house in a Pakistani-Indian area to a good-sized terrace house in a white working-class district. I immediately thought there had probably been some difficulty in the district; the father said he thought his son had had a spell cast on him! My immediate reaction was that here we had a psychotic father as well as a disturbed son, but I confined my outward speculations to asking whether the spell had been cast by the white people. His reaction was in one way reassuring as he told me that he knew that in my 'religion' we did not believe in spells but that Indians did do so. Apparently, when the family moved house they decided to become as English as possible—the children changed schools; they started to attend church, Sunday school, and the youth group. Apart from the fact that they received a great deal of criticism from their Indian friends, they were all very happy. Some months later, however, several Indians moved into the street and immediately pressure was put on them to become de-anglicised; the pressure was resisted and the Indian neighbours became more unpleasant, resulting in more disturbed behaviour on the part of the boy and the father's conviction that a spell had been placed on the family by the Indians. He was able to discuss the fact that the anglicised part of him did not believe this but the Indian part did so.

The problem of differential diagnosis is well illustrated here as is also the situation of too rapid acculturation as a symptom of inadequate personality development. Diagnostically, an important question here would be why the father felt he had to move at such a rapid rate in becoming acculturated that he alienated himself from his Indian friends. He was attempting to reject a basic part of his personality and to substitute a thin veneer of an alien culture. The significance of this problem might well be overlooked by a British social worker who, feeling that her pattern was the right one, might not question anyone's too rapid acceptance of such a pattern.

Obviously, this diagnostic confusion—resulting from work with persons from different backgrounds—makes it very difficult indeed to apply the basic casework precept of starting where the client is, since more often than not we do not know where he is! Additionally, like our clients, at moments of insecurity occasioned by such lack of knowledge, we will tend to over-emphasize our culture's ideals and may move into a more dominating role than is necessary, thus indirectly pressuring the immigrant to become British.

The caseworker who is prepared to seek out his own blind areas of prejudice and to allow the client his, may develop a relationship based on professional discipline and understanding which will ultimately enable the client to adapt to new demands and expectations. In this process, however, the social worker stands to gain as well. The solution of culture conflict is never a matter of one-sided adaptation but rather a process of partial and unequal but always reciprocal assumption of respective cultural traits.[1] In other words, the social worker changes too and his own cultural pattern is enriched.

Ours is a Spartan existence with little time for real pleasure and enjoyment. A culture that allows no spooks, no ghosts, no sixth sense, is a much more sterile one than the rich one of

[1] Pollak, p. 88.

the Irish. 'Sad, sad—!', says a visiting African writer in a London pub, 'White people are the saddest people I ever saw. They don't seem able to have fun. They don't sing; they don't laugh. Very sad.'[1] While we are helping our African clients identify with us, we can perhaps identify with them and move towards a more exuberant sense of pleasure; not only ourselves but our culture will be the richer for it. Casework with immigrants offers us not the opportunity to receive into our society an alien group but, rather, the opportunity to participate in the development of a new social phenomenon.[2]

Culture is not static; it is always changing. To a considerable extent it determines what we are, but we, in turn, determine what it is to become. 'Every profession is not only a product of the culture but also a creator of culture. . . . In complex societies such as ours, the role of the active agent of change is frequently taken on by the profession.'[3] Our professional responsibility is to analyse our own cultural pattern, to enrich it by blending it with others where the wisdom and traditions are greater, and so move forward to a more stimulating and exciting environment. We have also a responsibility, out of our understanding of inter-cultural conflict, to educate public opinion about the difficulties involved for us as well as for the alien in the process of acculturation.

---

[1] Lewis Nkosi, 'The Blacks', *Observer*, magazine section (10 January 1965), p. 8.
[2] Pollak, p. 92.
[3] Ibid.

III | Immigrants, Social Work, and the Community

Juliet Cheetham[1]

The impact of large numbers of immigrants clustered in areas hardly able to provide adequate facilities for their indigenous population, leads to official concern and local resentment. That poor conditions in these areas are endemic, and not caused by the arrival of immigrants, is now well known to those who are anxious not to isolate and condemn the newest single factor in the situation. The Plowden Report,[2] Rex and Moore,[3] and E. J. B. Rose and his associates[4] have provided the kind of evidence which leaves this no longer in dispute. If blame is to be apportioned, there is no longer an easy scapegoat.

More recently, it is possible to detect the awareness arising from fear, not so much of the individual immigrant, but of the aggression and fury which are born when a group, increasingly aware of its value and power, is consistently deprived of most of the good things of life. The summer fear which annually grips the U.S.A. no longer seems so remote from this country. Some politicians and social workers are now pessimistic about the development of consensus and harmony between coloured minorities in the U.K. and the white population, and are beginning to think more in terms of the management of conflict.

[1] This paper is a revised version of an article that first appeared in *Alta*, the University of Birmingham Review (No. 4, Winter 1967-8).
Juliet Cheetham is a Lecturer in Applied Social Studies, Department of Social and Administrative Studies, University of Oxford; she is a former probation officer for Lambeth and Brixton. She is the author of *Social Work with Immigrants* (London, Routledge & Kegan Paul, 1972).

[2] Department of Education and Science, *Children and their Primary Schools* (London, H.M.S.O., 1967). Chairman: Lady Plowden.

[3] J. Rex and R. Moore, *Race, Community, and Conflict* (London, Oxford University Press, for Institute of Race Relations, 1967).

[4] E. J. B. Rose *et al.*, *Colour and Citizenship* (Oxford University Press, for Institute of Race Relations, 1969).

Anxieties about Meeting Immigrants' Needs

There is still a minority who believe that to talk about a problem is to define and crystallize it beyond hope of solution. There is always the hope that if things are left unnoticed and unattended they will in some vague, indefinable way sort themselves out. There are also those who fear that looking at problems presented by immigrants will, by acknowledging differences, somehow imply prejudice. It is now known that all too often this worthy, misguided, perhaps frightened attitude means that many immigrants are left uncatered for. That a few immigrants quickly and successfully adapt to British society is a token too eagerly seized on by the complacent. The fact that special needs must be met by special services is avoided, firstly, because this is sometimes seen as the first step in the road to apartheid and, secondly, because minority groups only rarely succeed in becoming priority groups. This is due, in part, to a lack of political pressure and, less obviously, the fear of giving to a needy minority what cannot be given to a less needy but jealous majority. There is no easy answer to this, and it is not simply a problem of meeting the special needs of immigrants. Our Welfare State is increasingly faced with the dilemma of providing a thin layer of margarine for all, as of right, while it is clear that many are capably providing themselves with jam and some are struggling for bread. That everybody should have everything, without the qualification of need, is a fading dream. But the ghost of the means test has not been laid and it is right to be apprehensive of a means test being also a colour test. However, it is now widely agreed that a *laissez-faire* policy which either deliberately ignores or hopefully evades problems, be they concerned with immigrants or not, is doomed to disaster. There is an increasing demand for action on the part of the responsible authorities.

The Lack of Information about Immigrants

Public awareness of immigrants does not imply accurate knowledge, particularly the knowledge arising from prolonged personal contact. This is not surprising when the opportunity to meet and mix with immigrants is usually limited to certain areas. While many have been medically cared for by immigrants or had their tickets punched by them, there are still few who can claim to have talked at length with them, to have visited their homes, to have experienced with them the variety of feelings and emotions that are part of social relationships. Some would claim intimate knowledge as the result of being the neighbours of immigrants. Unfortunately, given the present housing situation, many people with this experience live in the twilight areas where the generally low standard of facilities makes the struggle to maintain decent standards particularly hard. Immigrants are then frequently, and utterly unfairly, seen as the source of all problems.

It is also well known that those who work with immigrants may, given an economic recession, fear that their presence, their willingness to work at any job in almost any conditions will threaten their own security. And while immigrants tend to fill the most menial and poorly paid jobs, it is tempting for some to see them as occupying the only place in society for which they are fit.

Who else can claim a wider knowledge of immigrants? Amongst the bidders there will be teachers and social workers who, depending on the areas in which they work, could rightly claim prolonged and intimate knowledge of some immigrant individuals and groups. Although social work has many shortcomings (and some of these will be considered later), it is worth looking at the experience and knowledge which social workers could usefully share with the wider community.

The Experience of Social Workers as a Contribution to Understanding

Social workers are primarily practical people. When working with immigrants they are constantly confronted with problems, the solution of which raises all the general difficulties already cited and can often be seen as a microcosm of larger issues. No one would claim that social workers are always successful in their work, but they do at least believe that some human problems are amenable to solution and they have some experience which proves that this is true. They can, therefore, say something about the most helpful ways of working with some of the problems involving immigrants and the origins of some of these difficulties. Secondly, if social workers are honest, they can use the experience gained from the failures in their work. Some of these obviously arise from lack of experience in dealing with unfamiliar situations. However, since social workers are part of the general population and subject to the same shortcomings, some of their failures are the result of attitudes and misconceptions shared by the community.

To understand the approach of social workers it is necessary to look briefly at the basic attitudes underlying modern social work and the direction in which this work is developing. Social workers believe in the intrinsic worth of each individual. Florence Hollis writes: 'We are guided in the help we offer by our value assumptions that man and his fulfilment are intrinsically valuable, that men are mutually dependent and bear responsibility for each other, that men are equal in their essential value and rights. . . .'[1]

Social workers know that most people at some time in their lives are faced with problems which cannot be coped with alone. Only a small proportion of these problems are actually brought to social workers, although recent literature on social pathology calls for more and better trained social workers to work with an increasing variety of social problems.

Social workers know that the individual in difficulty may have to cope with inner and outer needs. For example, a period of unemployment may mean that a family finds it difficult to manage its finances. The strain of having to cope with increasing debt and an inferior standard of living makes itself felt in the relationship within the family. The father and bread-winner may experience the insecurity and bitterness of a loss of status in his family; he may be painfully aware of his inadequacy as a provider. He may seek to reassert his position by inappropriate control over his adolescent children who may well be experiencing a bewildering complex of feelings towards him, ranging from anger to pity and compassion. In an attempt to improve the family finances, his wife

[1] F. Hollis, 'Principles and Assumptions Underlying Casework Practice', an address given at Bedford College, London, 1952.

may take a part-time job and thus strain her health. The fact that she can work while her husband cannot, may increase his feelings of inadequacy and frustration. He cannot, therefore, give his wife the support she needs, and so further resentment grows. No one would maintain that this sequence of events is inevitable, but it is an example of the complex interaction between material and emotional difficulties.

While it is possible to see certain patterns of behaviour, social workers believe that there is a need to study each individual and his problems before attempting to offer help. They know that different kinds of help will be needed and that no two people will use this help in identical ways. In looking at people's problems and in trying to work towards a solution, social workers realize that behaviour cannot be fully explained or predicted in terms of common sense. Emotions, very often coloured by very early experiences in the life of the individual, exert a strong influence on thought and behaviour, and it is assumed that how a person feels is going to determine in a considerable measure what he thinks and how he acts. While material need is very real in large numbers of families and no effort should be spared to alleviate this, it is not enough to expect that improvements in material conditions will mean that all problems will be solved, nor even that there will be an immediate response to this type of help. These then, very briefly, are the beliefs which will influence the social worker's approach to individuals in need. They can lead to a deeper understanding of problems and thereby a greater sympathy with the people presenting them, and are thus especially valuable in work with unfamiliar groups. These attitudes underlie the methods of social work which will be looked at later in this paper.

Before examining the nature and range of social work with immigrants, it is important to answer two possible criticisms or false conclusions. The first is that a paper such as this implies that the majority of immigrants need the help of social workers and that this assumption is, in itself, in some way derogatory. While it could be argued that if there were more social workers concerned with problems of adjustment to new communities many immigrants might face fewer difficulties, there is no evidence that social workers have disproportionate numbers of immigrant clients. Secondly, others may argue that the conclusions of this paper have only limited application as they are drawn from work with immigrants with serious social difficulties. The answer to this criticism is that while there are, of course, immigrants with serious long-term difficulties, the fact that someone may be helped on occasions by a social worker does not mean that he belongs to a special group. Indeed it could be argued that immigrants are faced with so many problems of material and emotional adjustment that it is the exceptional person who could not, at some time, be helped by the services of a social worker. Given the perennial shortage of social workers, however, whether he actually receives this help or not may depend on chance.

Some Problems Familiar to Social Workers

Those who have described the plight of immigrants in this country have concentrated on their practical difficulties such as finding accommodation and employment. A study[1] of their day-to-day lives often reveals conditions of great hardship. The total earning power of the family will be used to its limit to meet heavy financial burdens, including fares, high rents, and money for the support of relatives in the homeland. Many immigrants are at the mercy of unscrupulous profiteers, and there often seems little material gain for the long hours worked. However, this has been the fate of immigrants through the ages, and—while there is no desire here to condone these conditions—it is arguable that they are partly expected and accepted by many of them.

However, these are by no means all the difficulties with which immigrants must contend. There are others which involve personal and family relationships and usually come as a bitter surprise. It is important to understand these problems as they provide a new dimension to the difficult lot of immigrants and thus make apparently strange behaviour understandable.

Problems Posed by Immigrant Children

It is not at all uncommon for many immigrant families to experience acute difficulty in their relationships with their

---

[1] See Rose *et al.*

children. This is not peculiar to coloured immigrants. Irish and Jewish immigrant families have met similar difficulties. These problems can be divided roughly into two types: those arising from the necessary pattern of life of many immigrant families and those concerning adaptation to a new culture and environment.

The migratory process makes unusual demands on a family. In many cases it means that it must be temporarily split as the father arrives first and can only send for his wife and children after establishing a home. Moreover, where the cost of travelling is high, it is not usually possible for all the children to be united with the family at the same time. Some may be left in the care of relatives and money sent for their keep. There is no doubt that parents regret having to split their families in this way, but the practical difficulties of travelling and establishing a home can mean it is inevitable.

However, as the report *Immigrants and the Youth Service*[1] points out, the results of these separations can be very disturbing for the children and their families:

A child may arrive to find brothers and sisters born in this country, established as members of a family in which he feels an outsider; or he may arrive with only the faintest memory of his parents, who may have left him as an infant and whom he now has to begin to live with as virtual strangers. Again, before arriving here a child may have been lovingly cared for by his grandparents or other close relatives or, on the other hand, been rather casually looked after in a large and less closely related family. In either case, the newly arrived child will have problems of adjustment. He may miss those he has left behind and who, for much of his life, have represented parental authority and love. His departure may have been a shock to him, as it is not at all uncommon for children to be given only a few days' notice of their departure for the United Kingdom. He may have had little idea of his destination, for it is unusual for immigrants to receive any clear or helpful description of the country they are coming to. Whatever have been the particular circumstances of the child before his arrival in this country, it is likely that, partly depending on his age and the length of the time he has been separated from his family, he will be both confused and upset. He may have been given rational explanations,

[1] Youth Service Development Council Committee, *Immigrants and the Youth Service* (London, H.M.S.O., 1967), p. 18.

but these may not have been grasped by a child who feels shocked and insecure. Immigrant children, like the war-time evacuees, carry the memory of separation with them for a long time. He may still not understand why his parents, when they left for the United Kingdom, chose to leave him behind, and particularly so if they took others of their children. Equally, after he has become accustomed to them, he may wonder why he has been suddenly separated from his substitute parents. He may thus come to regard both his being left behind and his subsequent move to England as punishments.

It is easy to feel sympathy with children who have had these experiences. However, their parents, too, are in a difficult position. Many have made great financial sacrifices to bring their children to this country. It can be a bitter disappointment to find them confused, resentful, and withdrawn instead of grateful and delighted by their reunion.

These initial difficulties are increased when both parents, in their need to work long hours, have little time to be with their children. The struggle for material well-being leaves little energy left for talking to, and playing with, children who may become more and more withdrawn until both parents and children begin to feel bitterly misunderstood.

A Specific Case

Anthea, a seven-year-old West Indian child, faced many of these problems. She came to England when she was six after having lived with her grandmother in the West Indies since she was three. Her parents now had a two-year-old son who was placed in a nursery during the day. They both worked extremely long hours, the father as a foreman and the mother as a ward maid. They had heavy financial commitments including repayment of their fares and a rent of £8 a week for two rooms. The parents, who had looked forward to the arrival of Anthea, were distressed to find her uncommunicative, ignoring, whenever possible, both them and her brother. She appeared uninterested in the expensive clothes her parents had bought for her and her mother was angered by her careless treatment of them. She was particularly anxious that both her children should appear to the neighbours well turned out. Anthea got on fairly well at school but her teachers were sometimes alarmed by her vacant expression, her tendency to stare into space. She was a difficult child to reach, and her mother described vividly how she and Anthea would stare at each other in silence.

When Anthea finished school she was meant to go to a neighbour's until her mother finished work. However, after about three months in England, she began to wander off on her way back from school. Her parents would notify the police and then search for Anthea who would often be found hours later sitting in a park or asleep on a bench. She would not be able to explain why she had wandered nor what she had done. No one could doubt the dreadful anxiety Anthea's parents experienced during these disappearances and it is not surprising that they felt angry with their daughter for this apparent ingratitude and the shame they felt when police and social workers became concerned with them. The ritual of Child Guidance Clinic, Care or Protection proceedings, and the supervision of the Children's Department were only partially successful. The grief Anthea felt for her granny and her anger with her parents for apparently deserting her in Jamaica and then replacing her with a son, became clearer. But the anxiety and shame felt by each parent put a strain on their marriage. The wife, dutifully, but resentfully, gave up her job, but Anthea continued to wander. Her parents felt that 'the Government must take her' both as a protection and a punishment. And yet they were ashamed and disappointed at their mysterious failure to be accepted as good parents. Even though the social worker had a very good relationship with Anthea and her parents, even though a workable arrangement was made whereby Anthea was in a small children's home during the week and with her family at weekends, there remain scars of the wounds which were, for this family, the inevitable result of migration.

Older Children

Anthea, by going to school in this country, will grow up in a predominantly English environment. While this means she will be faced with the clash between two cultures, she will have some idea of the expectations that English people have of her. This is not the case with one particularly unfortunate group of immigrant children, that is, those who come to England when they are fifteen and have left school. Carol Ann, a fifteen-year-old girl from Guyana, was sent for by her mother, partly, it was suspected, because she had become too much of a handful for her grandmother. She was half excited, half frightened by what she found here. Her mother, who had been unmarried when Carol was born, was terrified lest she should 'misbehave'. She demanded all Carol's wages in return for keep and ordered her to be in by 6 p.m. every night. At first Carol submitted to this. She was, after all, completely ignorant about the ways of this new country. She still wore her native costume, and her English was hard to understand. The only work which could be found for her was boring and repetitious, the ideal background for her active adolescent fantasy life. She dreamt of becoming another pop-singing Millie. She found a boy-friend who gave her English clothes. She stayed out late (in her mother's opinion). She did not take her boy-friend home. She refused to give her mother all her wages. All this would seem fairly normal to English parents but Carol's mother was both furious and scared. It is true that her attitude towards her daughter was somewhat Victorian, but it was also true that she had reason to fear for Carol's safety. If she had been in Guyana, Carol would have accepted that she could only have a very limited contact with boys and that to do otherwise would seriously compromise her. It is not altogether surprising that her mother screamed 'You will turn her into a prostitute!' when a probation officer tried to persuade her to adopt a more liberal attitude. Carol remains resentful of her mother's attempted control, is confused by the freedom she envies, and wonders what is expected of her by her boy-friend. It is unlikely that it will be easy for her to find someone with whom she can happily settle down. It is also likely that she will be extremely unsure about how to bring up her children in an almost foreign country. Similar difficulties will arise when Asian girls—who are at present teen-agers and protected within their families in traditional ways—marry and in bringing up their families, are inevitably involved more closely with the British way of life.

Difficulties in Adapting to a New Culture

Carol's problems, although intensified by her unfamiliarity with England, also highlight the difficulty immigrant parents can have in understanding British standards of child care and discipline. To many English people, immigrant parents epitomize the best and worst elements of Victorian family life. As part of a cultural inheritance, it would never be easy to drop these standards to meet the demands of another culture, and many immigrants have no wish to do so. They are unimpressed by what they see of the results of English child-rearing practices. The spectre of rebellious delinquent children haunts them, particularly as they know that in this country they are on trial. To survive, they and their children are dependent largely on public acceptance and approval, and every immigrant knows that both of these are in short supply.

The immigrant child, however, particularly if he has had an English education, sees himself on an equal footing with other youngsters. He resents the rigid authority and control his parents try to exert. He is indignant about the corporal punishment which is still common in many immigrant families. He sees no reason why his parents should see his free time not as an opportunity for him to indulge in the usual leisure pastimes of teen-agers, but as an opportunity for further education. It is easy for him to be seen by his parents as rejecting his whole family, their standards and hard won position. Some immigrant children realize that in their desire to be the same as English children they have the support of their teachers, youth and social workers, and their friends' parents. All these people may regard immigrant parents as:

too strict and authoritarian—even unfeeling. They may also come to realize that some members of the community are strongly critical of immigrants' attitudes and way of life. These opinions may not be stated openly, but children are quick to sense unspoken attitudes and thus feel acutely the pull of two sets of adults who, perhaps unwittingly, have become rival influences.[1]

While it is very common for adolescents to feel alienated from their parents, this is usually a temporary phase. There

[1] Youth Service Development Committee, p. 21.

is evidence, however, that many immigrant children are beginning to despise their parents, thinking of them as not only conservative but backward and ignorant, very often the reason for their children's failure in a competitive and increasingly segregated world. Sometimes parents are also despised for being black. There are young people who dream of marrying into white families, of having white children. Beverley, a West Indian girl of nineteen, is on probation. Her parents are separated and she has spent some time in a children's home. She maintains fiercely that her father was white (although her mother denies this) and she has two illegitimate children by West Indian fathers. The children are in care, and Beverley feels very acutely her failure as a mother. Nevertheless, she realizes that she is so unsettled that she could not provide them with proper care. She is anxious to be accepted by white men, but so far this has only happened within gangs on the verge of criminality. Her current boy-friend is in Borstal. She is being steadily courted by a successful young West Indian student, 'But he is black', she says fiercely. She refuses to live with her mother, 'because then we are all black'. Not surprisingly, her relationships with her family are tense and they are now refusing to support her when she gets into trouble.

A seven-year-old child, under the supervision of the Children's Department, was asked to choose a Christmas present from a range of dolls which had been given by W.R.V.S. There was an equal number of black and white dolls. With no hesitation she seized a white one: 'I don't want an Indian —I want the clean one.' Turning to her Child Care Officer, she said: 'Oh Miss, I hope I have white babies.'

Niki, as he insists on being called, is an intelligent fifteen-year-old Indian boy. He is doing well at school but is cynical about his chance of getting a good job. His parents, who do not speak good English, think he will have a professional position. Niki, who knows more of the English way of life than they do, is beginning to despise their short-sightedness. He spends long hours in the public library, and is irritated by the customs and religious practices of his parents. He has a half-hearted attachment to a Youth Club but despises the main activities of the immigrant members which are weightlifting, cricket, and singing. He narrowly missed being taken to court when a youth leader found him quietly making a bonfire of his homework and school-books in the cloakroom of the club. While his parents are still ambitious for him, they are beginning to be impatient and fearful of his attempts at independence. They can discuss their bewilderment and anxiety only with each other and their Indian friends—many of whom are faced with similar problems.

The Position of Social Workers

There is, as yet, very little in the education of social workers which prepares them for the special difficulties of working with immigrants. There is, however, much in their traditional method of approach which is helpful.

Broadly speaking, in their work social workers adopt four main principles. The first is that experience has shown that it is of little use to criticize, exhort, beg, or directly teach people to change their behaviour. While they realize that much of it may be unacceptable to the community or the source of unhappiness to the individual and his family, they believe that it is rare for individuals to choose to do evil happily and deliberately. The first need is to accept the individual in a spirit not of criticism but of understanding. It is in this way that the second principle of social work can be put into effect: social workers hope that in seeking to understand rather than condemn the individual the beginnings of a relationship can be forged between them and those who need help. It is only in an atmosphere of trust and respect that people can begin to look at their problems honestly and try to find solutions which are both possible and acceptable to them. Only those solutions which develop from within—rather than those imposed from without—are of lasting effect.

A great deal is said today about the need for good relationships between management and workers, between teachers and the taught, between the white community and the immigrant population. Social workers cannot claim to have invented the beneficial use of good relationships, but they have considerable experience in communicating with groups of people who are alien to the general society. They are not immediately put off by hostility, reserve, or suspicion. Experience has shown that given time, patience, and understanding, contact can be made with most individuals, thus creating the possibility of forming relationships.

Thirdly, social workers are now concentrating their work not so much on the individual in isolation but as a member of a family. It is increasingly realized that it is only by understanding and working with the interaction of the members of a family that problems can be fully understood and solved. Where family bonds are strong, as in the case of many immigrant families, this is clearly of great relevance. British social workers are also following the American trend of working with groups of people who share common problems.

The fourth principle involves the increasing amount of time social workers spend in linking those in difficulty with the community. 'Community care', the familiar battle cry of contemporary social reformers, does not just happen. Somehow the community has to be helped to understand and accept its members who are in difficulty, and someone has to help those who have experienced rejection by the community not to see this as a continuous experience. This part of a social worker's job, as yet only partially developed, may be of significance in forging links between the immigrant and white communities.

The immigrant family in difficulty may find in a social worker someone who values them, and is really concerned for their well-being. The social worker does not resort to endless criticism and direction, and with her efforts and those of the family, a relationship may develop whereby family problems can be discussed, better understood, and coped with. This will sometimes involve the social worker in attempts to interpret the community to the family and the family to the community. It may also mean that some social workers will help immigrants to join or create the organizations and pressure groups which have a part to play in the solution of the problems of minority groups. However, it is foolish to deny that, while many social workers have found it very rewarding to work with immigrants, they also face unsolved problems.

Since this paper was first published, it has become clear that local authorities and social workers are becoming increasingly involved in community development and community action. While most community workers will be involved in helping groups of people living in deprived areas to identify their common problems and work for their solution, either through self-help or through pressure on the authorities which control resources, it is possible that some community workers may involve themselves especially with coloured minority groups which have particular problems. However, there is as yet practically no literature which describes this kind of work in the U.K.

Difficulties of Social Work

Some of the social worker's difficulties inevitably arise out of ignorance and this can quickly lead to misunderstanding. However, understanding the values and ways of life of their immigrant clients will not solve all problems.

While social workers are probably not as condemning of deviant ways of behaviour as the 'man in the street', they necessarily represent certain standards. How far, for example, can immigrant parents have a free hand in the discipline of their children when this may mean resorting to frequent, fairly severe corporal punishment or, as in Carol Ann's case, rigid rules and expectations of behaviour? How far can a blind eye be turned on situations which may be an inevitable result of an immigrant family's financial position? For instance, the shortage of places in day nurseries means that some children are cared for rather haphazardly during the day by neighbours, perhaps being left alone for a long time. While it is easy to decry these things, what alternative can social work offer? Concern for the emotional well-being of children and economic considerations have resulted in a very great reluctance to separate children from their families. K. Fitzherbert[1] thinks there are special reasons why extra efforts should be made to resist taking immigrant children into care. Many West Indians, in particular, see 'care' as good. They are not fully alive to the tensions which may arise in the future between them and their child if 'the Government takes them', as it is very often put. Additionally, it is

[1] K. Fitzherbert, *West Indian Children in London: A Study of the West Indian Family and the Child Care Service* (London, Bell, 1967).

increasingly difficult to find suitable accommodation for any children in care, particularly immigrants. As it is likely that an immigrant child, whether fostered or in a children's home, will be cared for by white people, the different expectations and standards to which he will become accustomed will make his eventual reunion with his family even more difficult.

The Problem of 'Fairness'

Immediately, in working with immigrants, social workers are faced with the problem of fairness. Is more to be tolerated, resisted, controlled just because a family is coloured? There is obviously no easy answer to this question although perhaps something can be learnt from the case where a probation officer was discussing, patiently and permissively, with a coloured mother her attitude to her daughter's misbehaviour. The probation officer felt the girl was only behaving in a way which was normal for her English friends. Her mother, however, was adamant in her demands for total obedience, emphasizing that in their homeland this misbehaviour would not be tolerated. Suddenly the probation officer lost her temper, saying sharply: 'Well your daughter is an English girl now and you must accept that she will behave like other English girls.' Rather unexpectedly, perhaps only because a basically good relationship existed between the probation officer and the mother, she smiled broadly, asking excitedly: 'Do you really think she can be English?'

While some administrators, politicians, as well as members of the general public, feel that immigrants may be helped by more direction and control, social workers are very reluctant to accept such an authoritative position. It strikes at the very heart of their principles. This is a very complex problem which has been lucidly discussed by B. Kent.[1] It is possible that the insistence and emphasis that social workers place on clients directing their own affairs may well be inappropriate when people are, through the stress of isolation and ignorance, in a particularly dependent state. Certainly the social work approach of discussion and consideration of all alternatives,

[1] B. Kent, 'The Social Worker's Cultural Pattern as it Affects Casework with Immigrants', *Social Work* (Vol. 22, No. 4, October 1965) ; and above, Chapter II.

in an effort to help a client make the right decision for himself, can be very strange for many immigrants. When white people have for generations been seen as semi-autocratic rulers, it is not easy to understand or accept the approach of the English social worker.

A further difficulty arises from the pessimism many immigrants have about their circumstances which for centuries may have seemed hopelessly fixed. The idea that one's situation may be amenable to change through one's own efforts, may seem unreal; and so social workers are often baffled by the fatalism, the dependence on 'the Government', the unwillingness to express opinions, which are all characteristic of some immigrant families. There are cases where real and deep relationships have sprung up even though these may have involved the uncritical dependence of immigrants on social workers. This has usually been a temporary but necessary phase while the immigrants grew more accustomed to a completely new country. There is, however, some evidence that coloured people, whether immigrants or not, are becoming increasingly vocal in their opinions about the social services. This presents another challenge to social workers.

There is now a good deal of debate amongst social workers as to whether special methods of working need to be learned and adopted in connection with immigrants. Those who believed there were no special problems are steadily being forced to take a fresh look at what they are achieving. There is evidence that some immigrants are confused by the approach of social workers, but before social workers abandon their customary approach it is worth emphasizing that while immigrants may, for a while, look for some direct control or advice, the 'expert-master/dependent servant' relationship is a very seductive trap from which escape is difficult. It would be dangerous if social workers forgot one of their main aims: to help individuals face and solve their own problems as independently as possible.

Problems of Communication

It is very fashionable to emphasize the problems involved in communicating with immigrants. This is not surprising when completely new languages have to be learnt by both parties and particularly so when one party is traditionally conservative in its contact with foreigners. Nor should it be forgotten that, language apart, the ways that different people express their feelings can appear strange. Extremes of feeling may be much more readily displayed by some people and when faced with this, many English people recoil. While it is important not to minimize these problems, they can become a shelter behind which the two groups can hide. To tackle them may hardly seem worth the effort, particularly when it is imagined that the immigrants' stay may only be temporary. The importance of studying immigrants' traditions is sometimes suggested as a stepping-stone to better communication, but this study can stop short of better communication, serving only to emphasize the strange differences of the immigrant groups. What may be forgotten is that groups do not remain static. There is a wish and a need for adaptation, painful though this often is, and this process needs to be more widely studied.

Further Difficulties Facing Social Workers

What has been said so far may imply that social workers are always able to face problems fairly and objectively, but social workers are not so inhuman as to be able to act so perfectly. Undoubtedly, immigrants and their problems present some threats to social workers, as they do to the rest of the community.

English social workers are reared and educated in a child-centred society where the emotional problems of children are increasingly recognized. One of the cardinal beliefs is the need for children to have a stable relationship with a mother or mother substitute during the first four or five years of life. However patient, however understanding the social worker, the continuous trail of children such as Anthea—the casualties of the immigration process—is a cause for concern and sometimes anger. On many occasions social workers can feel enraged by the apparent lack of concern or understanding shown by immigrant parents towards their children's emotional welfare. Immigrant parents are not, of course, alone in this, but in the struggle for survival some find it very difficult to see that there are problems other than material ones.

Equally, social workers, like the rest of the community, are distressed by some aspects of immigrant child care. The somewhat Victorian attitudes are a painful reminder of an age from which we have only recently emerged, when children and individuals often suffered acutely. In particular, women social workers find it difficult to work helpfully with some immigrants with marital problems. The empathy needed to work successfully often does not extend to those caught up in a marital tangle of obedience and disobedience, submission and even physical control. Some women who themselves feel only a shaky equality with men can feel threatened and infuriated by these situations.

The Search for Priorities

The special nature of the difficulties faced by social workers and the unfamiliarity of working with immigrants, will influence their decisions about allocation of their resources, in particular their time. The continual pressure on social work agencies means that while a basic service can usually be offered to most clients, some are selected, both consciously and unconsciously, for greater attention. It is probably true that the special problems presented by immigrants which seem strange and even threatening are given low priority. Happily, however, this is not always so. Apart from considerations of justice and expediency, which should weigh heavily with every social worker, there are those who are specially attracted to work with particularly deprived groups and those who are challenged by new problems.

Lessons to be Learnt from Social Work

The special knowledge that social workers can gain about immigrant families can help both private individuals and administrators towards a better understanding of them. Equally, social workers can help those who feel threatened by immigrants towards a better understanding of the foundation of their fears, a calmer appraisal of problems and their solution. Social workers are increasingly being used as a bridge between the individual and wider society, be this his family or the community. When their skills develop in this sphere, they could be usefully used to promote better relations between immigrants and the native community. It is not without significance that the Race Relations Board, when advertising for Conciliation Officers, sometimes asks for those with professional training or experience in social work.

Since it is now generally recognized that the special problems of immigrants may demand special, if not priority, services, there is the constant danger that separate provision, meant to meet a temporary need, may become permanent. This fear certainly stalks behind the policies for the crash teaching of English to coloured school children, which involve their being separated for long periods from the rest of the school. Social workers have long realized that when the provision of special services meant the isolation of the individual from the community, frequently more harm than good is done to both parties. Such is the case with the care of the mentally ill in prison-like institutions, the isolation of the old, and the separation of deprived children from their peers. Immigrants in England are not isolated in such drastic ways, but the experience social workers have in trying to handle problems within the community whenever possible is clearly relevant. This demands helping the individual in difficulty not to flee to the relative, but increasingly negative, security of the institution or to the group who share his problems but which is becoming increasingly isolated and paranoid. It also means helping the community to accept and tolerate things which may seem strange, perhaps undesirable but not, as a consequence, necessarily dangerous. As has already been indicated, social workers with an interest in community work may also be involved in working with the conflicts that can develop between majority and minority groups. Where large numbers of immigrants are faced with the prospect and perhaps the hope of increasing separation from the host community, those social workers who wish to become involved in this problem will need to have experience in aspects of community work, a branch of social work hardly developed in England.

Meeting the needs of individuals by setting them apart in groups sharing related problems, while at the same time not crystallizing their separation from the community, is a very complex problem. For instance, some probation officers have started discussion groups for the parents of children who are proving difficult to handle. It is felt that, partly through sharing their problems, these parents can give each other much support. It was known that in the one area many coloured parents were also having difficulty in handling their children. Their problems differed in many respects from those of white parents and the probation officers felt that these immigrant parents would not find the established groups particularly helpful. No doubt, too, they feared the disruption of the white groups and the creation of an all-too-easy scapegoat through the introduction of coloured parents. The question of setting up separate groups for immigrant parents was considered, but then there was the problem of what this separateness would mean to the parents. Possibly the probation officers were also afraid of leading a group which might be resentful and angry and where they would be, for once, the white minority. In the absence of special knowledge or experience, the groups were not formed and thus the needs of a group of parents with special difficulties were neglected.

When Social Work Seems Irrelevant

It is important for both social workers and the community to recognize the weaknesses and failures of social work as well as its irrelevancy in certain situations. Only in this way is it possible to avoid the pitfalls of imagining that social work can remove problems which go to the heart of society. In spite of all hopes to the contrary, social work is primarily concerned with mending rather than preventing.

Social workers have rightly been accused of attempting to get people to accept impossible situations and of being too cautious in their condemnation of appalling social conditions. This was particularly true when it was fashionable to focus primarily on the psychological rather than material needs of the individual. While this focus has now changed, it is still true that most social workers on the whole are not social reformers. Their necessary involvement with groups representing many different interests partly prevents this. In easing the distress of individuals it is sometimes quicker to fight small battles on their behalf rather than to attack directly the core of a more general social problem. Indeed, such an attack is usually quite beyond the resources of individual social workers. It is also true that many individuals may find it easier and more acceptable to adjust and conform to behaviour expected of them, than to fight expectations which may be unjust. This is one reason why social workers are often accused of being conformist and submissive to authority. While social workers possess information that can be of great value to those who wish to fight injustice and to improve the lot of immigrants, it is not likely that many of them will themselves as individuals take up the cudgels in an active and public battle. Social workers may, however, be able to create or join pressure groups which are working for the more equitable distribution of resources.

However, most social workers have very little experience of working with individuals and groups who are actively and aggressively attacking the society in which they live. To such people, social workers are the lackeys of the Establishment and, indeed, they may prefer this role to the lonely lot of a rejecting minority. This is proving a serious problem in the U.S.A. where social workers, black and white, are often finding it impossible to make contact with an increasingly disillusioned, righteously angry, black community. This problem is beginning to show in England particularly as second- or third-generation immigrants are themselves consistently denied the opportunities available to their white compatriots. The tolerant suspicion of the West Indian boy who used to challenge his probation officer with a cheery, 'Would you move house if I came to live next door?', has changed to a mute hostility and an insistence on bringing a number of coloured youths with him on his visits to the probation office, visits which are now made only because of his reluctant obedience. The experience of the last few years has shown that it is vital for social workers to be aware of the fact that to many coloured people they may seem actually or potentially hostile just because they are white. It is important for questions of actual or supposed discrimination to be discussed with coloured people however uncomfortable this may be for white social workers. It is possible that coloured social workers may have a special contribution to make in work with immigrants and their families although the automatic allocation of coloured clients to coloured social workers would be harmful.

The social workers who can make useful relationships with this new generation of coloured people will be exceptional. It is likely that they will have to adopt a new role and methods of working about which almost nothing is known in this country. Given the situation of many young immigrants and coloured people, their frequent disappointments and rejections in some areas, and their growing separateness from and hostility to the white majority, traditional social work can indeed seem irrelevant.

A West Indian boy who has been in touch with a child care officer for some years, sums up the situation well:

When I was sick for home you helped me say so. When I was mad with my parents you stood up for me and you stood up for them too. They quote you, you know Miss C; they say, 'Well if Miss C says so, it's all right'. When I was in the school play you came and my parents stayed at home. When I was looking for work you came with me and they didn't dare go on saying they had no more jobs. When I started going with Ann [a white girl] you spent a long time with my parents and with hers. When I was angry and lonely and when I was sick of all the tests people give you I came to see you. But when I see the rotten street where I live, when I talk to the other coloured people, when I got turned down for promotion, when Ann and I couldn't get a mortgage, when the local kids call Jim [their four-year-old son] 'dirty black and white bastard' there is nothing you can do—nothing! Then I want to fight and kick and scream and the only people who can help are my mates who feel the same.

IV | The Social Worker and the Young Blacks[1]

Gus John[2]

The advent of non-white minority groups to Britain and their presence within British society have posed a number of challenges to the social structure of this society and to the agencies which statutorily service it. Varying opinions have been expressed about the nature of this challenge. There are those who maintain, for example, that the social situation that now obtains as a result of the presence of immigrants is not unprecedented and that consequently the *status quo* could be upheld while the process of acculturation and settlement works itself out. Then there is the other, similar argument which says each immigrant minority group has its attendant social problems which are overcome sooner or later. It happened in the case of the Jews, the Italians, the Poles; it no doubt will be the same for the Asians and the West Indians. At an earlier stage it was also being argued that all would be well with the second generation of immigrants. 'Once they are born here', it was argued, 'and grow up in our society, go to our schools and [implicitly] do as we do, they will be all right and will help to build our integrated society.' But the fact is that feelings of frustration and a sense of failure characterize the lives of more and more young blacks in and out of school.

This kind of thinking has generally resulted in little adaptation of the conventional ways of doing things. A trial-and-error approach has been followed as a response to the needs or demands of black people. Some agencies, safe in the belief that what they offer is necessarily good, have chosen to turn a deaf ear or to become very defensive in the face of criticism about the deficiencies of their services. Among these are the

[1] The term young blacks is used to denote mostly West Indians who were either born in Britain or who came here while still of school age.

[2] Gus John is a Research Social Worker at Manchester University.

schools, the Youth Employment Service, the youth service, the police, and a wide range of social services. Very few agencies have actually developed the machinery to help identify the range of need as defined by clients themselves or to monitor the extent to which they satisfy such needs.

An understanding of the black community and its problems is dependent on a grasp of the social processes and dynamics of social interaction which are at work in that community; the term 'community', as employed here and in so far as it implies a homogeneous group, is meant to encapsulate the sub-groups, ethnic colonies, and sub-cultures which reflect the complex patterns of settlement in any one area of concentrated black population.

The nature of the relationship between the social worker and the young black person is determined by, among other things, their perception of each other as well as the young person's awareness of himself in relation to his particular situation which is seen as demanding social work intervention. In order to grasp the context within which he comes to an awareness of himself or within which his particular situation is actualized, we must first work towards an understanding of the young black person himself and of the various forces around him.

Background to Present Issues

The presence of the black young person in Britain might be examined within a context of social change. As a result of certain socio-economic changes within Britain, and correspondingly in Asia and the West Indies, Britain now has a sizable young black population. Their parents came in response to a need which might be considered reciprocal: there was Britain's need for a cheap labour force in great numbers in the 1950s and there was the immigrants' need for employment as well as their aspirations for a higher standard of living. For the majority migration was also an arrangement which, hopefully, would enable them to do their duty by their children.

The message communicated to the black community by Britain was that they were highly undesirable though indispensable. The immigrants' response to this was predictably ambivalent. Socialized in British ways as they had been, accepting British values, standards, norms, Queen, and flag, they sought to identify with Britain in almost every detail, only to find her a very reluctant 'mother'. On the other hand, there were constant reminders that the arrangement was made on purely economic terms and, therefore, any satisfactions should be seen in the context of economic rewards only.

The 'host' society opted to insulate itself from them, ascribing to all immigrants a working-class status and making it difficult for them to live in other than areas already bedeviled by multiple social deprivation. In this way it was possible to lump them as one with disadvantaged white groups and institute a new set of clichés: 'But, let's face it, it's not colour, is it? It's all to do with poverty and class.' 'Yes, but everything you say could equally be said about the white working class. Black and white are in the same boat here. It's all a matter of exploitation.' At the same time, the immigrants continued to bear the brunt of social inaction and were made to account for the existence of social ills which generations of the white working class were socialized into. Within this social context immigrant adults find very little to aspire to for themselves even when they are very highly motivated for their children. In spite of their rejection now of many British values, their home life and patterns of child-rearing reflect their acceptance of the terms the 'host' society has prescribed for them. Having accepted the limitations of their place within British society, they expect their children to accept the same and to look to the home and to the family for shaping their relations to themselves and the outside world. At the same time, they expect their children to gain status through upward mobility, and this in a society which they themselves regard as at once hostile, overpermissive, liberal, and racist. It is a source of comfort to many immigrants to tell themselves from time to time that some good day they will be out of it, they at least will 'go back home'. This becomes a useful psychological game since many admit, and even more know, that this is unlikely.

The Position of the Young Blacks

The immigrants' children, on the other hand, are here to stay whether or not they were born here, and are seeking to demonstrate they are also here to live *on their terms*, which are different from those their parents accept. This attitude is basic to an understanding of the young black who is not a 'second-generation immigrant', since this is a misnomer, but who also does not feel that he is a young black Britisher. This is because British society expects the young black to accept the terms that were written up for his parents and which the latter have largely abided by.

As far as the black youth is concerned, he is here in many ways despite himself, a product of an historic piece of social change. But for him this is his country and he is aspiring to live here as an equal citizen with dignity and respect, and with a mind—not just an athletic, sexually potent body. Unfortunately, the tendency in British society is to continue to regard him as it regards his parents. Its perceptions and expectations of him are the same and he in turn is expected to relate to British society and its institutions in the same way as his parents did. Stereotypes are employed, myths are perpetuated, and the young person is not allowed to break out of this cocoon.

At home his parents exhort him to work hard and to do better than the rest because he is black. Their every other word to him is 'success', 'success', 'success'. Because of a variety of pressures at school he usually fails to perform to the best of his ability. His teacher may or may not be openly hostile, or may expect very little of him in terms of ability or performance, or worse he can be infuriatingly patronizing. At a recent in-service training course one teacher talked about the 75 per cent black population of a secondary modern school and remarked: 'Some of them are more intelligent than one would expect'!

Even when the young black succeeds he still finds he cannot presume that the jobs to which his qualifications entitle him will necessarily be open to him. His blackness is a handicap that he must live with. He rejects the aspirations of his parents because according to his analysis they are unrealistic

—unrealistic not for the reasons usually put forward by the experts, including the Youth Employment and Careers Advisers, but because upward mobility through education when applied to the black youth sets many on the path of frustration. The young black person continues to be at the mercy of the social forces operating in society in a particular way *vis à vis* the black man. Since his parents' terms are unacceptable to him and since he analyses his situation from a different vantage point, his adaptive measures for coping are of a different order from those employed by his parents.

The young black person in Britain feels neither British nor West Indian and is forced to evolve a culture that is peculiarly his. He therefore has to try to find an identity which can only be black, neither West Indian nor British. He seeks to understand himself within the context of the reappraisal of white society by black people, and notably by other young black people. He is not alone in his search for fairness and justice because of his blackness. He no longer chooses to accept white society's definition of him and to be self-effacing, deferential, aspiring after whiteness in order to gain acceptance. Rather, he is seeking to define white society for itself in the way that his parents feel they are unable to do. Black power, the resurgence and reaffirmation of black cultural identity, the growth of a distinctively black youth culture, all form the framework within which the black youth works out his stance to this society. He derives more support and guidance from this source than from any other. He sometimes finds himself in need of this support in order to come to terms with his own family.

Though this outlook contributes towards the 'generation gap' between the young black and his family, it is not the whole answer. The 'generation gap' is due to a much bigger problem and is mainly connected with the attitudes of the parents. In many respects these are Victorian in the literal sense and as such they differ from those of the most reactionary working-class whites.

Though the parents have been selflessly sacrificing and ambitious on their children's behalf, the latter have suffered greatly from the lack of real contact with their parents. Continued labouring under personal and social stress has made communication and rapport between parents and children very difficult. Most of the parents' emotional resources go into efforts to cope with their social situation rather than to foster rapport and understanding with their children. While such conditions invariably obtain for sections of the white working class, the fact that black parents grew up in a more supporting environment with a greater tradition of community care, makes adaptation to this social situation very complicated and costly in terms of their relations with their children.

Children born outside Britain and brought here after years of separation have usually missed out in relationships with their parents. Subsequently, many fail to develop a sense of belonging and closeness to their parents. When going through adolescence here, they fail to get the required understanding and support from their parents. Instead, they are often faced with very authoritarian attitudes and with strict controls, usually imposed without sensitivity by parents who did not share the growing up process with them and towards whom the children feel relatively little.

Unlike, perhaps, most other groups before them, young blacks by their presence in Britain create a new social situation which demands new adaptive mechanisms. This fact is generally overlooked to the extent that conferences are still being held at which social workers, youth workers, teachers, and youth employment officers, among others, discuss 'the difficulties of identification and adjustment of black teenagers'. The black youth is here considered to be non-adjustive or deviant in his stance towards white society. The assumption is that there is something normative and indeed static about British society that he must identify with or adjust to. Take for instance the youth service. Irrational liberalism, which thinks that to ignore differences is to remove them, spends its time bemoaning the fact that multiracial youth clubs don't work, arguing whether the notion of black youth clubs is admissible. In areas where an attempt was made to start multiracial clubs it was soon found that the moment one group moved in the other moved out. There is little evidence of clubs being able to retain two groups at once, except by accommodating them on different nights. Service, in this respect, has to act on the understanding that people's needs can be as different as their social situations.

British society continues to show itself to be not the most susceptible to change, expecting every minority group within it to adjust and identify with its values and norms. Many young black people reject these values and norms. Apart from being denied equal status and being made to feel 'outsiders', young blacks are exhorted by the family and the school, as socializing agencies, to aspire towards certain goals which they know they will be debarred from reaching. Many more question the assumed 'goodness' of these values and norms which they see as being employed to keep them at bay.

It is from this position that young blacks question the structure of British society and the institutions which operate within it. Too often, however, the response they receive is 'conform or else'. Parents admonish them to conform without having regard for their point of view or even crediting them with having one. Failure to conform often results in parental rejection. Teachers also expect young blacks to conform. Failure to conform results in their dismissal by teachers as either unteachable or wanting in educational motivation.

The Social Services and the Needs of Young Blacks

Large numbers of black young people are being defined as 'deviant'. Even more are being judged as failures. In trying to preserve or indeed build a favourable self-concept, the young person finds he is seldom able to transcend society's low opinion or low expectations of him. The over-all situation described gives rise to intense personal frustration. This kind of frustration is often translated into social conflict by the young person acting out the role of 'deviant' in which he is cast. An awareness of the stress and frustration experienced by the young black is crucial to an understanding of his perception of the social worker, youth leader, and others seeking to establish contact with him.

Social work, like policing and the other known forms of social control, is carried out within a social context and is usually guided by some form of social policy adopted to deal with the situation as it is perceived at the time. It should follow that as the situation develops or changes the social policy will be altered or radically reformed. I have posited developments within this society which have resulted in a new social situation demanding a series of new approaches, specifically related to the needs of black people and their way of defining their situation. Social work agencies, including the youth service, have seldom stopped to reappraise the social context within which they operate. This is because the existing system continues to throw up casualties in such numbers that agencies are perpetually involved in a servicing operation without stopping to consider the over-all social implications of their particular mode of operation. If the social worker fails to question the validity of the service he is offering in the light of the young black person's understanding of his situation, or indeed in the light of his appreciation of the social worker's professional role as a statutory agent, he can expect to find a series of responses none of which might be positive:

(i)   he could find himself being torn between the young person and his parents or between the young person, his parents, and his peer group or/and the black reference group with which he relates in the community and which might well determine the stance he takes towards social workers or welfare officers;

(ii)   he could also find that the service he offers acts dysfunctionally *vis à vis* his client and can be counter-productive;

(iii)   he might find himself offering a service in spite of, rather than on behalf of, his client.

Some social workers are not themselves happy about the services they offer. A few are talking in terms of working towards a radical alternative to social casework. The radical social worker must, however, accept that as far as the young black person is concerned his position becomes untenable. Such a worker is usually out on a limb and experiencing a fair degree of isolation. This sense of being alone is further accentuated when despite his efforts he is lumped with the rest. Not so long ago I was asked by one of these social workers: 'How does one go about establishing credibility with black teen-agers?' This worker felt he knew them well and they knew him well enough, but they never ceased to regard him as 'the man from the Town Hall', 'one of them', 'one of the Establishment', who despite being a good guy still had *the power to screw them*. This is the sort of ambiguity the radical social worker must live with if only because as the young black person understands it, to be a radical social worker and to be employed by agencies that they define as Establishment, is incongruous at the very least. By continuing to work within that system, the radical social worker is at least implicitly accepting the system's definition of social deviance. The young black person, on the other hand, feels that he is in a position to point the accusing finger at the system and its institutions and charge them with being violent towards him in a very real, physical sense. Because of this, many black youths take probation officers and social workers for a ride and are consequently called 'con men' or 'smooth operators'. But it would be misleading to dismiss them as such. What they are trying to say is that they do not accept the system's definition of deviance or delinquency or 'problem teen-ager' as it is applied to them and, therefore, are prepared to argue with the consequences of their being so defined and categorized.

Socail work needs to be client orientated in the real sense, necessitating an acceptance of the person's definition of his situation on his terms, albeit in a contextual sense. It demands a reappraisal of such concepts as deviance, adjustment, teenage delinquency, among others. The facility with which the adaptive measures employed by young blacks, in response to their situation, are dismissed as deviant or non-adjustive, invariably makes for self-fulfilling prophecies. Instance, for example, aspects of the relationship between police and young blacks, and the attitude that a number of blacks grouping together is synonymous with trouble; or the feeling that young blacks can be expected to be carrying drugs or knives. While no one would suggest that the police have no cause to be concerned about aspects of life within the black community, there is nevertheless ample evidence to suggest that because of their expectations of trouble and tension, fracas have sometimes been precipitated. Instance, too, the difficulties experienced by groups of black people in hiring halls or renting schools' premises because proprietors expect that their halls will be smashed or that there will be some come-back from neighbours because of noise.

The question of colour makes for differences in the relationship between the black person and the white social worker which warrants further consideration. The nature of this relationship will largely depend on:

(i) the extent to which the white social worker brings to bear his values and standards on the black person's situation, or employs acquired attitudes and prejudices in his relations with the black person;

(ii) the degree to which he as a white social worker is identified with the rest of white society which the black person sees as hostile or oppressive;

(iii) whether or not the social worker is client orientated, concerned not with perpetuating the 'them-us' dichotomy but with making the system work in the client's favour, encouraging him to make demands and increasing his awareness of his rights within the system.

The black person's experience of social workers is often one in which the social worker is judging, condescending, superior, if not utterly condemnatory, and unsympathetic to the just demands clients make of them not as individuals but in their capacity as workers within the system. The black person has also to put up with occasionally expressed hostile attitudes such as this social worker's response to a mother of four: 'Don't expect the Children's Department to take your children off you. They are your responsibility—no one sent you to go breeding like some guinea-pig.' This woman was unemployed. Her common-law husband, the father of the four children, had deserted her some months earlier. Social Security had suddenly stopped her benefit one week, advising her to go out and find work. The eldest child was five, the youngest seven months. She elicited this response as she inquired about the possibility of having her children boarded out while she found work. She hated the thought of 'going to Social Security'. She had never done so before and certainly would not have contemplated it but for the fact that she had no means of support. Other attitudes I came across personally were: 'You people come to this country and expect things to be done differently for you'; or 'What I cannot understand is this business of "beating" children, even teen-age girls. It really is a most barbarous habit. It is about time parents were taught that children have certain rights in this country'; or 'Before you go on about the way this society gives the black youth a raw deal, why don't you do something about their parents who give them an even worse deal. They not only reject them and chuck 'em out for the slightest misdemeanour, they even expect us to have them put away.'

In the present climate of bitterness and frustration among young blacks, white social workers need really to enter the black person's situation if they are to be accepted. In the case of a black social worker, even if he comes wearing 'a black skin in a white mask', the young black or his family will try to identify with him despite himself. (After all, part of the alienation black youths experience results from the attitude of black professionals and black intellectuals.)

One of the peculiar functions of black people in British society is—in the process of speaking to ourselves about ourselves—to present to British society a critique of itself. The main body of the thesis developed in this paper has been that the black young person, out of an understanding of the unique nature of his situation, is seeking to define on his terms what his relationship is to Britain. The role of the black professional, such as social worker, teacher, psychologist, is to examine individually and collectively how the institutions within which each person operates relate to black people in the community. The black professional functions as a vanguard, an enabler, an educator. He is in a position which entitles him to know how the system works and to pass that knowledge on in the community—for part of the powerlessness that the disadvantaged suffer stems from a lack of knowledge not only of their rights and how to exercise them, but of the vulnerability of the system itself. Part of the all-inclusive politicizing function is to convince people that those who run the system don't necessarily know best and that the system is not impregnable. Looking for the deficiencies in the services offered is not an intuitive process. It demands a certain degree

of knowledge of what the services offered could be and ought
to be.

It is significant that the major issues on which some stand
has been taken by the black community in Britain have cen-
tred almost exclusively around the position of young blacks.
The black community is beginning to accept that British
society and its institutions will not, indeed cannot, respond to
young blacks' definition of their needs, and is consequently
taking up the issue with them. For example, the problem of
the number of West Indian children being sent to schools for
the maladjusted or the educationally subnormal has been
a cause of great concern to the black community for some
years. The tide took a particularly evil turn when in Haringey
in 1969 the local education committee published plans for
busing, streaming, banding, and branding which horrified
black parents and community workers. As a result of the
fight waged at that time, the Caribbean Education and Community Workers' Association was formed to examine the
various aspects of the education of black children, and particularly the problem of E.S.N. schools. Black educationists
and community workers are now concerned with working
with parents and groups of young people. The black community is engaged in taking care of itself by initiating its own
community care programmes which, far from seeking to
absolve the system of its responsibilities, give black people the
confidence and knowledge and bargaining power to demand
that the system accept those responsibilities and carry them
out according to the needs of the black community as defined
by the black community.

Conclusion

Social work cannot help but take cognizance of the fact that
a new process is in operation in practically every black community and on differing scales. The black community is
becoming increasingly aware of its needs and is prepared to
put up a struggle to have them met. Equally, the young
blacks are no longer prepared to accept for themselves the
status and conditions defined for their parents. This developing situation creates a new social context within which social

work needs to be done. Social policy may choose to ignore this fact but the social worker cannot. In the long run, the individual social worker must choose whether or not to be indicted with the system.

V | The Fostering of West African Children in England *

June Ellis[1]

A kind foster mother wanted for two Ghanaian children, boy 2 years, girl 1 year.
Foster mother required for 6-week-old Nigerian baby girl.

There is a great desire for foster-care amongst West African students in Britain and these advertisements are typical of those to be found every week in the *Nursery World*, in news-agents' windows, and in local papers in and around London. At present there are more than 5,000 children of Common-wealth students[2]—the great majority from West Africa—who are in private foster homes, or whose parents, like those quoted above, are seeking homes for them; although most children are in foster homes in the London area, they are increasingly being placed further afield.[3]

In her useful article, Pat Stapleton of the Commonwealth Students' Children's Society discusses the difficulties these students are likely to meet when trying to make arrangements for the care of their children in this country; she describes some of the problems that may arise because of the differences between their culture and ours. As far as I know, this article is the only one of its kind, and of the relatively few other

* This paper has been reprinted from *Social Work Today* (Vol. 2, No. 5, 3 June 1971).

[1] June Ellis is a Lecturer in the Department of Social Administration, University of Birmingham.

[2] P. Stapleton, 'Children of Commonwealth Students', in the Institute of Race Relations *Newsletter* (January and February 1969).

[3] There are about 900 West African children in foster homes in Kent and more than 250 in Hampshire; see Stapleton. Recent research into private fostering in a Midlands county has found that of 143 children in private foster homes, 61 per cent were West African; see R. Holman, 'Private Fostering: An Approach to Research and Some Initial Findings' (University of Birmingham, 1970).

references to West African family life, most are to be found in specialist journals and books. It is probable, therefore, that workers who come into contact with these student-parents and their children, know little about West African culture. This is unfortunate because without a knowledge of the West African background, misunderstandings are likely to arise; sometimes, for instance, West Africans may be classed with West Indians, whereas their situation and problems are quite different.

It is because of the lack of information in this field, and the obvious need for it, that this paper has been written. I have made use of writings on family life and methods of child-training in English-speaking West Africa, as well as my own observations there. Though there are inevitable shortcomings in the data, it is hoped that this paper will provide some insights into West African life; an attempt will be made to answer the question that most British social workers would probably want to ask: why should so many West African students want to have their children fostered?

From our point of view, it is disturbing that young children who have parents who apparently could look after them, are placed in foster homes, even if these are good. But, of course, foster homes are not always satisfactory, and some of these West African children, who are almost all under five, may pass through a succession of homes in a comparatively short time. For example, K, a Nigerian girl, had been in twelve different foster homes by the time she was five and, not surprisingly, had serious behaviour problems; O, a three-year-old Nigerian girl, became very destructive and did £20 worth of damage when she had been in her sixth foster home a week or two; J and R, a brother and sister who had been in a succession of foster homes, were, at two and a half and four, in poor health, apathetic, and withdrawn.[1]

Pat Stapleton writes: 'Paediatricians in London have a growing number of cases of severe deprivation among coloured foster children.' She also quotes a London psychiatrist who described a little Nigerian girl as the most disturbed two-year-old he had ever seen.[2] Though these may be extreme

[1] Cases from the files of the Commonwealth Students' Children's Society.
[2] P. Stapleton.

examples, there are many cases where the care that the children are getting seems inadequate. Despite adverse experiences, however, there are many more student-parents who want foster homes for their children than can at the moment be helped, and there are others who continue with fostering even though their children seem to be running the risk of severe damage. Why is it that presumably intelligent parents put their children at risk in this way?

Viewing the Problem in Context

The difficulties that these student-parents face—the problems of finding accommodation with children, the extreme shortage of nursery and day-minding facilities, as well as the special problems to be faced by those, like nurses, whose training requires that they should live in—should not be underestimated; they are very real.[1] But even allowing for these difficulties, in many cases fostering is not something which is forced on these parents because other possibilities have failed, but rather it results from a positive decision on their part: they want their children fostered. This readiness to see fostering as a solution—rather than choosing one of the alternatives, such as day care, or even deciding that the wife should stay at home and be a full-time mother while her husband studies or undergoes training—may seem puzzling; and it is easy to regard such behaviour as irresponsible or selfish. However, if it is viewed in its West African context, and not within our usual European frame of reference, this same behaviour acquires quite a different significance and becomes easier to understand.

Fostering is a widespread traditional practice in West Africa. It is not merely something which becomes necessary because of a crisis, as in the West; fostering of this sort is, in fact, only an insignificant part of the whole. Most fostering occurs for reasons which are socially defined and which fall short of any situation whereby the parents are unable to care for their children. Just as the care of the children is shared amongst a number of adults in the traditional compound

[1] See P. Stapleton.

5

where an extended family group lives, so also the sharing and exchange of children are practised when the family is physically separated. A recent study of the Yoruba of Nigeria (the largest group of West African parents seeking foster-care for their children in Britain)[1] found that 20 per cent of the children of householders interviewed in Lagos were not living with either of their parents, and 25 per cent of the households were caring for the young children of their relatives. The author comments: 'the exchange of children between relatives is an accepted custom. . . . So children are likely to spend some of their childhood living away from home.' In another study of the Yoruba, it was found that the thirty élite households in the sample had a total of eighteen children of relatives living with them.[2]

The Ibos of Eastern Nigeria have also been found to practise fostering. In a study of Ibo village life,[3] it was noted that 'children spend a certain amount of time staying away with relatives, and the eldest son and daughter of a couple are supposed to spend a good deal of time, as children, with their paternal grandparents, as compensation to these for loss of their son at marriage'. Nor is fostering confined to Nigeria. In Ghana, 'children are often lent for shorter or longer periods to help in the house or on the farm of a relative, or as a mark of respect to an elder, or to receive some special kind of training, or to benefit from being brought up in a literate household'.[4] Amongst the Gonja of the North, 'there are commonly agreed-upon rights of kinsfolk to take children and rear them apart from their own parents . . . and there are sanctions on refusing to send children to be fostered'.[5] Although fostering is institutionalized to an unusually high degree amongst the Gonja, it is also common amongst other Ghanaian tribes. In a study of over 300 Ga children, it was found that 25 per cent

---

[1] P. Marris, *Family and Social Change in an African City* (London, Routledge & Kegan Paul, 1961).

[2] B. B. Lloyd, 'Education and Family Life in the Development of Class Identification amongst the Yoruba', in P. C. Lloyd (ed.), *The New Elites of Tropical Africa* (London, Oxford University Press, 1966).

[3] M. M. Green, *Ibo Village Affairs*, 2nd ed. (London, Frank Cass, 1964).

[4] B. Kaye, *Bringing up Children in Ghana* (London, Allen & Unwin, 1962).

[5] E. Goody, 'The Fostering of Children in Ghana: A Preliminary Report', *Ghana Journal of Sociology* (Vol. 2, No. 1, 1966).

were living apart from both parents,[1] and fostering has been reported amongst the Ewes and Fantes too.[2]

More Diffuse Sharing of Children

Part of the answer, then, as to why West African students turn to fostering in this country, is that fostering is a traditional part of their culture. Instead of the more or less exclusive parent-child relationships we know, there is a much more diffuse sharing of children amongst relatives. Of course, this 'cultural acceptability' of fostering, important and necessary though it is when seeking for an explanation of the fostering that West African students do here, does not entirely explain why parents, traditionally used to the sharing of children with their kin, should be ready to place their children with strangers; there must be additional factors to be taken into account.

It is necessary, first of all, to appreciate the great importance of education to the West African—it has even been likened to a passion[3]—and how essential it is that, given the opportunity of acquiring an education, nothing should stand in the way. In West Africa, where differences in income are very much greater than here, virtually all the well-paid, prestigious jobs require a high level of formal education. Peter Marris has said, and with only slight exaggeration: 'Nothing can be got without it, but with it anything is possible.'[4] However, it is often not merely a matter of individual achievement; years of dreaming and saving by the entire family may precede the student's journey abroad and he will be expected, on his return, to contribute to the family and will probably help to pay for the education of younger relatives.[5] So for the student, who is likely to be older than his English counterpart, the prizes are high but the pressures are great.

[1] J. Ellis, 'Child-training in Ghana with Particular Reference to the Gas' (University of Ghana, M.A. thesis 1968).

[2] See E. Goody; and K. A. Busia, *Report on a Social Survey of Sekondi-Takoradi* (London, Crown Agents for the Colonies, 1950).

[3] M. J. Lasky, *Africa for Beginners* (London, Weidenfeld & Nicolson, 1962).

[4] P. Marris, *African City Life* (Uganda, Transitions Books, 1968).

[5] J. C. Caldwell, 'Extended Family Obligations and Education: A Study of an Aspect of Demographic Transition amongst Ghanaian University Students', *Population Studies* (Vol. 19, No. 2, 1965).

While one can readily appreciate the importance of success and the student's intense desire that nothing should prevent him from getting the necessary qualifications, it is perhaps not quite so obvious why, in such a situation, students' wives should also be working or training whilst their young children are being cared for by others. Why do they not stay at home and look after them? In Britain this is what we expect will happen and the mother (particularly one having small children) who goes out to work is likely—even if she does not encounter overt expressions of disapproval from others—to feel a sense of guilt and to wonder if she is perhaps failing in her 'true' role. But this is not generally so in West Africa; despite the much larger families, it is the working mother who is the norm and it is unusual to find mothers who are not involved in some kind of gainful occupation. In a study of the Yoruba,[1] it was found that 90 per cent of the wives of the householders interviewed were working, mainly as traders. And working is not confined to uneducated women: of a sample of thirty élite mothers of five-year-olds (and some of these women could reasonably be expected to have a younger child also), 80 per cent were in full-time employment.[2]

Women's Traditional Role as Traders

Because of their independent income, women are able 'to help members of their own family of origin—they would send money to their parents, help educate the children of their brothers and sisters without any obligation to consult their husbands'.[3] The Ga women of Ghana, who live in and around Accra, are also well-known traders: 'Besides trading to convert her husband's goods into money or some necessary commodity, every [Ga] woman carries on some sort of trading on her own account.'[4] Although this was written thirty years ago, things seem to have changed little in this respect; a recent study of over 300 Ga school children found that only 7 per cent of their mothers were not working.[5] And amongst the

[1] See P. Marris, *Family and Social Change* ...
[2] See B. B. Lloyd.
[3] P. Marris, *African City Life*.
[4] M. J. Field, *Social Organisation of the Ga People* (London, Crown Agents for the Colony, 1940).
[5] J. Ellis.

Akan of Ghana, the women in the rural areas were traditionally farmers, sometimes working their own land as well
as their husbands'; increasingly, with urbanization, they have
turned to trade. In Koforidua, an Akan town, it was esti-
mated that on one market day at least 70 per cent of the adult
female population were engaged in trade.[1] It is also noted
that 'town women are under a compulsion to trade. There is
an expectation that women will support themselves even after
marriage and that they will contribute to the support of the
children.'[2]

Clearly, the woman's role as indicated here, involving a
status and independence that are linked with her economic
activities, is somewhat different from that in our society.[3] If
we recognize that the woman will probably expect, and be
expected, to support herself, to at least contribute to the support of her children, and to help relatives too, then it follows
that the kind of pressure that influences a male West African
student is also relevant to her situation. Thus, her desire to
work or to undertake some kind of training is very great;
sometimes courses are available here that are not offered in
West Africa, but even where a similar training (for example,
for nurses, seamstresses, or hairdressers) is available at home,
the *cachet* attached to British training is so great that it would
be hard to resist the opportunities that are here.

Of obvious relevance, too, in this examination of the question of fostering are the attitudes of West Africans towards
children and the methods of child-training they use. Children
are greatly valued in West Africa. They are seen to be the
major, perhaps the only, purpose of marriage,[4] and are an
important source of social prestige. 'Childless adults have
little or no social status; they are not invited nor expected to
comment on public affairs. They are accorded no respect by

[1] D. McCall, 'Trade and the Role of Wife in a Modern West African Town',
in A. Southall (ed.), *Social Change in Modern Africa* (London, Oxford University
Press, 1961).

[2] Ibid.

[3] And it may be different in other parts of West Africa, for instance, in the
Moslem North. However, Northerners are likely to be only a very small proportion of West Africans in England and so do not significantly affect the arguments advanced.

[4] A. Phillips (ed.), *Survey of African Marriage and Family Life* (London, Oxford
University Press, 1953).

either relatives or strangers and are equally despised by young and old.'[1] Further insight into these attitudes is gained from a report on the Tallensi of Ghana[2] who were 'either sceptical or appalled' when told that Europeans may deliberately refrain from having children. And amongst the Ibo, 'Celibacy is thought not only unnatural but immoral, for it is a person's duty to his descent groups to carry on the line and maintain the strength of the lineage and clan'.[3] Such considerations may be especially important for the parents of a student and may lead them to urge their son or daughter to start a family even when studying abroad. It is therefore not surprising that given this kind of cultural orientation and pressure, West African students in England have children when, from other points of view, it would not seem to be in their best interests to do so.

Strictness in Child-training

Although socialization techniques obviously vary from tribe to tribe, traditional West African methods of child-training tend to be severe.[4] At first, however, the infant occupies a very privileged position in society: he is loved, indulged, and close to his mother for most of the day (probably on her back while she works). This care and concern make good sense where infant mortality rates are high. But, once the child can walk and talk, quite severe demands—that is, severe in terms of European expectations—are made on him. The whole nature of his environment changes (and this change is often associated with the coming of a new baby): he is no longer looked after mainly by his mother but is handed over to the care of others in the house or compound, perhaps siblings, and as one of many children, he is soon expected to help with tasks in and around the house. Discipline is strict, and the

---

[1] B. Kaye.

[2] M. Fortes, *The Web of Kinship among the Tallensi* (London, Oxford University Press, 1949).

[3] P. Ottenberg, 'The Afikpo Ibo of Eastern Nigeria', in J. L. Gibbs (ed.), *Peoples of Africa* (New York, Holt, Rinehart & Winston, 1965).

[4] See P. Marris, *Family and Social Change. . .*, and B. Kaye. Also, B. B. Le Vine, *Yoruba Students' Memories of Childhood Rewards and Punishments* (Ibadan, Ibadan University Press, 1962). (Occasional Publication No. 2.)

'good' child is one who is respectful and obedient. This strictness, at least amongst the Ga tribe which I studied, seems to be associated with a pessimism about human nature: the child is seen as one who is not naturally good but whose impulses must be curbed. Spoiling is looked on with great disfavour and 'there is a general belief that parents are not the best suited people for the upbringing of their children; they tend to pamper their children making it impossible to exercise that little bit of hardness, if not harshness, that Gas believe to be an essential ingredient of the socialization process'.[1]

This kind of rationale may lie behind the traditionally strict upbringing found amongst different societies in West Africa and, to the extent that it is widespread, it may help to explain the way in which West Africans can accept the fostering of their children with strangers and, more particularly, bad fostering experiences. I am not arguing that they like the situations their children are in, or even that given an absolutely free choice, many would not wish to care for their children themselves; rather, given a general outlook in which adversity is seen to be a necessary part of child-training, then it becomes possible to rationalize apparently stressful experiences as being good for the character. One must remember too, and this is very important, that what is perceived by us as undesirable may not be defined as such by a West African, who may find the kind of psychological insights that are everyday currency to the educated person in Britain irrelevant or very hard to accept. Long, intense, continuous relationships are not so likely to be a normal part of his family experiences; discontinuities probably are. *151996*

It is important to consider how far this discussion has relevance to élite as well as non-élite West Africans. Most of the studies referred to have been based on 'traditional' groups, and, clearly, if the élite are Westernized to such an extent that traditional values and pressures are no longer very important, then much of the force of what has been said will be weakened. However, I do not think this is so. It would be wrong to assume the same kind of horizontal stratification of

[1] G. Mills-Odoi, 'The Ga Family and Social Change' (University of Ghana, M.A. thesis 1967).

society that we know in Britain, or to suppose that one can think of an élite as being rather clearly distinct from the rest.

Sense of Loyalty to Tribe and Kin

Kinship is of prime importance, and the differences in wealth and occupational status that undoubtedly exist are to be found within families to an extent that is unknown here. It has been observed of Ghana that:

there are as yet few conventional barriers of the kind existing in Western industrialized societies. The sense of loyalty to both tribe and kin, as well as the feelings of dependence on these, remain sufficiently strong to ensure the persistence of frequent personal contacts . . . among people of widely disparate status levels.[1]

And of the West African élite in general, it has been said that: 'the present élite—or those well on the way to attaining this status—have been and are still being drawn quite substantially from the poor and ill-educated masses'.[2] It therefore seems likely that the differences between the élite and non-élite may not be as great as their positions on the social scale would indicate and that only a small fraction of West African students here are likely to be so Westernized that traditional norms and values have little relevance for them.

Here in Britain we rightly see much to concern us about the fostering of West African children. The Commonwealth Students' Children's Society is working to improve standards of foster-care and is making efforts to get parents, where possible, to make arrangements for the day care of their children. But the pressures towards fostering are so strong, and the viable alternatives so scarce, that fostering is likely to continue. This being so, it is helpful if we can look at it from the students' viewpoint: they want a service for which they are willing to pay; they do not feel that they are doing anything wrong, indeed by gaining qualifications they may

[1] G. Jahoda, 'Social Aspirations, Magic and Witchcraft in Ghana: A Social Psychological Interpretation', in P. C. Lloyd (ed.).
[2] P. C. Lloyd, 'The Study of the Elite', ibid.

see themselves as serving the long-term interests of their children and wider families. This is not irresponsibility; their responsibilities and loyalties may be different from ours, but they are still responsibilities and loyalties.

VI | Mental Health Problems in Pre-school West Indian Children

G. Stewart-Prince[1]

I have worked in Child Guidance Clinics in London for more than fifteen years. Only recently have children under the age of five come to us in any number and these are mostly West Indian. In this age-group we now see more West Indians than any other children.

General practitioners, Health Visitors, and others who care for these children are coming to realize that there is something wrong with many pre-school children in West Indian families.

A few of these children have problems of the same sort that English children have—disturbances of feeding, sleep, behaviour, and so on. But most of them present a picture that I think does not occur in English children (or in Scottish, Irish, or Welsh). It seems to be something specific to the West Indians—possibly, although I am not quite sure about this, specific to West Indian children in this country.

Typically, the mother complains to the Health Visitor or family doctor that the child takes no notice of her, though she feels that he hears what she says. The mother, or frequently the father, may be afraid that the child is mentally defective or mad, but the parents often have a good idea that he is not.

The mother frequently has a feeling that the child does not wish to respond or does not find it sufficiently rewarding to do so. She may say, 'He don't want to know', or 'He don't give me no heed'.

At first sight the syndrome smacks of autism, but I don't think it is the same thing.

[1] This paper has been reprinted from *Maternal and Child Care* (Vol. III, No. 26, June 1967).

Dr. Stewart-Prince is Consultant in Child Psychiatry at King's College Hospital, London.

Look at a typical case, the Murray family. Donald, age three years and four months, was referred to the Child Guidance Clinic because he made no effort to communicate with his family or with others, and a paediatrician suspected that he was autistic.

He was slow in walking and retarded in speech. He could say 'Mum', and his mother had taught him to count up to six, but he made no effort to communicate. In addition, he wet the bed, refused the pot, messed his pants, and still insisted on drinking from a bottle.

His mother felt that he understood what she told him, but, in her own graphic words, 'He doesn't pay you any mind'. He showed marked jealousy of his toddler sister and pulled her forcibly from his mother's lap. Donald could not co-operate in formal mental testing, but his mother's report on his social development gave him a 'Social Age' of two years.

Mrs. Murray brought Donald and the two-year-old Mary to the first psychiatric interview. She was an elderly mother, neat, intelligent, and forthcoming. Both her children were beautifully dressed, Mary in particular; she looked like a solemn angel in a blue silk dress, with white bonnet, socks, and shoes. Mother placed Mary on the couch before accepting my invitation to take a chair, and for the hour-long interview Mary remained there motionless. (One suspects that she is developing the same condition.)

When I had the opportunity after nearly half an hour to approach her directly and try to interest her in dolls and toys, she made no response; the impression she gave was of overwhelming apathy. Donald showed no anxiety at coming into the room, and did not acknowledge my presence. For the first ten minutes, as his mother talked, he stood inert and withdrawn and stared vacantly into space. This is very unusual in European children who come to the clinic.

He eventually picked up a small motor car and a wooden crane which he handled without making any attempt to play with them. I approached him, holding out my hand for the toy, saying that he might like to play cars with me. For the first time he showed emotion, scowling angrily, and pulling away his hand as if he feared that I would wrench the car from it. He turned back to the cupboard, replaced the crane, and banged the car on a shelf. This negative response made it pretty certain that he was not an autistic child.

Eventually he dropped the car, clutched the seat of his pants, made grunting noises and wriggling movements, and I showed Mrs. Murray where to take him. Most three-year-olds would have asked, in words, for the toilet. While they were gone I made my unavailing attempt to contact Mary.

Mother and Donald returned and she continued her story. Donald from time to time handled a variety of toys. He didn't play with them but he always showed resentment if I tried to join him.

Mrs. Murray's story and her state threw some light on Donald's symptoms and behaviour pattern. She soon revealed her depression and despair, and talked of her exhaustion in trying to bring up five children under the age of nine in two rooms on a limited income. She showed nostalgia in talking about her country of origin, and guilt in telling me about the seven older children she had left behind there in the care of their maternal grandmother.

Partly to contribute to their upkeep, she works in a canteen from six in the evening until six in the morning and, not surprisingly, she finds it difficult to tolerate the babyish demands that Donald makes on her—increasingly since the birth of little Mary.

In 1966 we saw twenty-three West Indian pre-school children in the clinic and twenty-one of them had this syndrome. They were aloof, apathetic, withdrawn, scarcely speaking or speaking not at all.

This may not be the only big mental health problem found in these children because there are certain specific reasons why they come to us. General practitioners and Health Visitors naturally suspect that such children may be deaf or mentally defective, so the children come to us via the audiologist or the paediatrician. None of our cases was deaf, in fact, but of the twenty-one, nine had never developed speech, five were said by their mothers to have acquired a few words and then lost these (usually after some disturbing event such as separation from the mother or the birth of a new baby), and seven had acquired a little speech, inadequately and slowly, but made little use of it for meaningful communication within the family.

The Question of Autism

So marked was this feature of failure of communication that many of these children were suspected of suffering from Early Infantile Autism. I think it is doubtful whether this label, which was originally applied to a small group of children of sophisticated American background, is relevant. But four of our twenty-one children were diagnosed as autistic and a further six showed 'autistic features' such as mutism, preoccupation with objects and rhythmical activities.

The Question of Retardation

Sixteen of the group of twenty-three were suspected of being mentally retarded when they were tested by the techniques appropriate for a child of indigenous parents of similar age. However, for many of these children, communication difficulties threw doubt upon the diagnosis; in addition, many had definite histories of maternal deprivation and of gross lack of intellectual, emotional, and social stimulation which suggested that the apparent retardation might be of complex origin.

Factors in the Children's Histories and Backgrounds

Traumatic early separation from the mother

Seventeen of the twenty-three had been separated from their mothers for at least one month and most of them for a good deal longer. Some had experienced grossly inadequate care and multiple fostering. In some, the father had also been separated from the child for a substantial period—a factor of importance to the child, but one less easy to relate to the clinical picture.

Depression in the mothers

No fewer than twenty of the mothers were assessed as being

clinically and often quite seriously depressed. By this it is not meant that they were showing understandable reactions to the worry of their child's problems and to other domestic and familial stresses, but that they were ill in themselves.

In many, the illness was of long standing. It often produced slowing of their mental and physical processes so that they were sometimes mistaken for unwilling or unintelligent informants. Sleep disturbances, loss of appetite, marked irritability, and feelings of inadequacy and hopelessness were other common features. It can easily be seen how such a condition greatly increased their difficulty in coping with a young, difficult child and with their other problems.

Some of the factors in this maternal depression seem fairly clear: homesickness, feelings of isolation in their neighbourhood, disillusion with the quality of their lives in this country, and marital conflict are frequent factors.

One possible, more specific, causative factor requires further exploration. Ten of the depressed mothers on coming to this country had left behind varying numbers of children, usually in the care of the maternal grandmother or aunt. These mothers were struggling with considerable feelings of guilt at having had to leave their older children.

This factor often imposed a heavy financial burden on the family in this country because money had to be sent back for the maintenance of the children and, sometimes, was also saved up in the hope that the older children might be brought here to join the family.

Should the family succeed in saving up sufficient money to bring to England one or more older children, this could produce various mental health problems in these older children when they rejoin their mothers; but description of these problems is beyond the scope of this paper.

Structure of the family in this country

In only five cases was the patient the only pre-school child in the family. Two mothers had four children under the age of five, eleven had three such, and nine had two. When this is considered along with the problem presented by the disturbed child and the fact that in some cases the other children also had symptoms, the demands made on this group of mothers are easy to imagine.

Mothers at work

Fourteen of the mothers in the group were working. This may not differ greatly from the figure for the indigenous population, but there seem to be important qualitative factors.

Many of these mothers stated that, with all their other burdens, they found their work so exhausting that they felt unable to give to, or to enjoy, their children. Some, like Mrs. Murray, were out at work from evening until morning, and on their return home could manage only to feed their children before retiring to bed. A few were struggling heroically to combine an all-night job with a part-time one in the afternoon.

Inadequate housing and financial difficulties

These two sets of factors are taken together because, from the clinician's standpoint, they proved to be so intertwined as to be incapable of separate evaluation. Thirteen of our families suffered from such difficulties.

The complexities of these environmental factors may be gauged from the elaboration of an individual case. These parents, with three children under the age of five and great financial difficulties, lived in one room. They did not allow the children out, partly from fear of the traffic and partly because they felt the neighbourhood to be hostile.

Both father and mother felt a sense of guilt towards the children and realized that they were offering them restricted, unstimulating, and unchildlike lives. They tried to deal with this by buying them expensive toys they could not afford, tending to choose toys beyond the comprehension of the child concerned.

In the case of the three-year-old, they gave him a large pedal car which he was not strong enough to manage and which he could hardly have operated in the space available.

This may illustrate the way in which psychological, cultural, economic, and social factors interact, and serve to underline the need for a multi-disciplinary approach to these problems.

It also brings us back to the title of this symposium: 'The Pre-school Child in the Immigrant Family: The Challenge of his Early Development'. The challenge seems to be on two main issues: namely, how do we try to assess his needs, and having done so, how can we attempt to meet them?

We in the clinics are concerned with the individual child or the individual family, but the problem—and the challenge— is really social, economic, and political. We do not yet know its full nature and extent. Overwhelmingly we need more knowledge, more research.

I believe that the children's psychiatric clinic must play a role in this research, but that this role is limited by the fact that it is difficult for the mothers we have been considering to get even once to a clinic. And it is difficult for us to be sure that the 'patient' they bring is the only one with mental health problems.

Useful research will have to be based on visiting the families at home and it will involve a wide range of professions. It will be expensive, though certainly cheaper in the long run than ignoring the problem. Society must face the challenge.

VII | Conclusions

J. P. Triseliotis

The Cultural Factors

Individual personality, as well as family relations, appears to be shaped by the many-sided psychosocial and cultural processes which operate in any given culture. These processes vary from one culture to another but studies suggest that there are generic aspects which permeate all cultures. This genericness is observed in biological, social, and psychological phenomena. Although some tendencies are generic, they are likely to appear to a much greater degree in some cultures than in others. What is important in one culture becomes unimportant in another, or what is 'proper', 'good', 'positive', 'indicated' becomes 'improper', 'bad', 'negative', 'contra-indicated' depending on the way people perceive their social environment and their values. For instance, the Greeks consider that *philotimo* (love of honour) is not only the highest Greek value but the highest value *per se* and therefore they are more *philotimoi* than people of other cultures. The British may hold similar views about 'privacy' or 'fairness'.

As people nowadays, more than ever before, travel and interact with others outside their groups, perhaps they do not feel so strongly and so exclusively bounded by their own group's values, but these are still very important to them. To be brought up in one culture and then suddenly to be confronted with the values of another, in itself creates difficulties and conflicts. It is for this reason that external pressures aimed at the assimilation or integration of immigrants generate undue anxieties and conflict among the new-comers. These pressures also reflect adversely on a society that cannot tolerate cultural pluralism and distinctiveness. The process of uprooting and resettlement is painful enough for many immigrants without added pressures to conform or integrate. The apparent politeness, smiles, or conformity of most immigrants often hide considerable unhappiness resulting from the loss of relations and friends and from the process of adaptation to a new environment.

No doubt the process of immigration by its very nature infers some readiness on the part of the immigrants for some kind of accommodation of values, provided that accommodation takes place within an atmosphere of mutual respect and toleration. Immigrants in Britain do not exist in total isolation and ignorance of the larger society, but their outside social contacts are very limited, which makes any kind of mutual understanding difficult. No doubt the impact of large numbers of immigrants has suddenly brought the average member of the local community into direct confrontation with values, customs, and tendencies hitherto unfamiliar to him. This has often sparked off prejudice and intolerance and has led to open or discreet forms of discrimination in housing, employment, education, and other spheres. Intolerance resulting from cultural conditioning and political agitation tends to limit appreciation and understanding of the newcomers and their ways of living, and polarizes feelings.

It would be fair to add, however, that most immigrants have experienced little hostility or outright rejection from their white neighbours and schoolfellows. They are more aware of indifference and aloofness which they feel are worse. In the factory they mostly have fellow-countrymen as their only immediate work-mates, and at school there is little mixing between immigrant children and local ones. There are very profound cultural differences, especially between immigrants from the East and the local population. It would therefore be naïve to underestimate the tremendous difficulties that exist on both sides when considering the building of bridges. Some of the cultural differences and attitudes are very deeply ingrained; immigrants from the East show great distaste for English habits of behaviour and English people have similar feelings about the immigrants' eating, cleaning, religious, and other habits. Even with the best will on both sides, which at the moment is not much in evidence, it will be a long time before some form of comfortable integration is achieved. Dislike and prejudices are not confined to those between coloured and white British. Similar to the West

Indian inter-island dislikes is the discrimination and hostility shown by Indians and Pakistanis towards people from a different caste, religion, or linguistic group. The more educated and upper-class Hindus or Moslems here are often critical of their less fortunate fellow-countrymen.

It is recognized that the host country has a right to specify minimal standards of values and behaviour which it can tolerate but that the immigrants, too, have a right to choose for themselves the most comfortable mode of accommodating themselves to their new environment. Coloured immigrants have suffered most from varied forms of discrimination and their life here has not been easy. They have often been exposed to additional stresses that may have had deleterious effects upon their capacities to function adequately as wage-earners, parents, and citizens. The positive contribution of the Black Power movement in fostering pride in black people is to be welcomed, but some of its adherents can be criticized for laying more emphasis on people as black, rather than people as people. Maybe after so many years of oppression and discrimination this reaction was to be expected.

Socio-economic Factors

Immigrants as a group are playing a fair part in the economic development and the welfare of Britain, though their social conditions rarely reflect this contribution. As a group they are economically and socially vulnerable and, perhaps, more at risk than any other comparable local group. They generally live in some of the most disadvantaged and culturally deprived areas, facing considerable hardships. The social deprivations they are experiencing may not be dissimilar to those experienced by the more underprivileged members of the host community but most immigrants have the additional handicap of being coloured. Yet it would be grossly misleading to equate the immigrants with the more underprivileged members of the host country because the reasons for their situation are not the same. Many of their social problems are peculiar to their situation and are not the result of personality difficulties, physical or mental disability, or family dysfunctioning, which may be the case with some of the local underprivileged groups. A very interesting picture which illustrates this point emerges from the Grieve[1] report on homelessness in London. Of the immigrant families among the homeless, only 10 per cent of those evicted by private landlords were made homeless as a result of rent arrears, compared with 33 per cent of other groups; marital breakdown accounted for 13 per cent of the applications from British and Irish families but for only 7 per cent of the Commonwealth-born homeless applicants; only 8 per cent of the Commonwealth-born homeless were unemployed at the time their application was recorded, compared with nearly 25 per cent of the British and Irish homeless.

In fact, comparing the current situation with the 1962 report on London's homeless, the report says: 'It is these immigrant families who now conform most closely to the typical family becoming homeless in London ten years ago—then identified as "ordinary decent Londoners." ' In other words, coloured immigrants are more likely than whites to be full-time workers, loyal husbands, and good rent-payers evicted by landlords. Who would have thought that immigrants would ever be described that way?

Traditional social work is of limited value in combating vast areas of social and cultural deprivation—areas encompassing shortages of suitable housing, poor social, health, welfare, pre-school play and educational facilities. These areas of deprivation can only be tackled through the implementation of massive programmes of social development. It would be naïve to forget that resources will always be limited and subject to claim by other groups. The planners of social policy are faced with the challenge of apportioning extra resources that can be used to discriminate in favour of all disadvantaged groups, including immigrants. Traditional arguments for more surveys do not seem to hold true any longer; areas requiring priority measures and extra resources have been identified—housing; more pre-school facilities because more mothers are going out to work; schools geared to compensate for the deficiencies of home and environment and geared to an understanding of the multi-cultural background of children —and the disadvantaged have been defined.

[1] S. Grieve, *Homeless in London* (London, Chatto & Windus, 1971).

The implementation of programmes aimed at improving social, educational, and other facilities in disadvantaged areas will inevitably raise aspirations, which could lead to considerable frustration and disillusionment, if immigrants or their children find that opportunities are not open to them. The success of all such programmes will inevitably depend on how far the immigrant community comes to feel equal in a climate where neither racial nor ethnic background is seen to be the arbiter of their future.

There is need for economic and other help for black youth groups. The small self-help coloured groups initiated by the young people themselves or born out of their parents' anxieties, are not enough. The youth service has done little to face the challenge set by the problems of coloured adolescents. The service itself has few resources and these need to be considerably increased and expanded in an imaginative way. The Community Relations Commission in its annual report for 1970–1 urges that a greater attempt be made to meet the increasing demand for short-term facilities designed for particular groups. The report goes on to say: 'This would give the coloured adolescent a better opportunity to identify with his peers and with astute leadership and objective programming, social contacts between white and coloured youngsters could be fostered and developed through outside interests.'

Community relations, particularly relations between the police and the black community, need to be improved. In some areas of the big cities considerable tension exists between the police and black people. Tough and efficient law enforcement takes little account of the social situations that lie behind many patterns of law infringement. Some police officials are certainly concerned about this and it is hoped that means will be found to disperse the atmosphere of mistrust and suspicion that many young members of the coloured community feel.

Other measures could take the form of programmes of social education among immigrants to help them to understand their basic rights and obligations as citizens. The complexity, for instance, of the social services, which is beyond the understanding of many local people, is entirely incomprehensible to the vast majority of new-comers. In addition, such procedures as house purchase, hire purchase agreements, rate and rent rebates, and the operation of tribunals could be put across to them through their own developing institutions and by enlisting the co-operation of their emerging leaders. Voluntary work has a lot to contribute in this area. Immigrants also lack a point of reference outside their immediate family and cultural group, and a great amount of preventive work could be achieved by familiarizing them with such institutions as their local Citizens' Advice Bureau or Social Service Department. Similarly, the potential of the school, an institution with which most immigrants are familiar, could be used as a reference point for socialization and the early identification of possible difficulties. The value of the schools as prophylactic centres could be considerably increased, especially if serviced by social workers who can follow up enquiries or reach out to immigrant families through their children. There is encouraging evidence, for instance, which suggests that even the more isolated Asian women can be allowed by their menfolk to attend programmes, such as classes in English, when these are very small, personal, highly specialized, and run by women.

Social Work Contribution

Social workers have a big contribution to make by helping to identify need where it exists and by exercising pressure on the system, both from within and from without, to take notice of that need and do something to meet it. If they are to succeed in influencing social policy in this way, social workers will have to replace the traditional consensus model with a more radical one, and demonstrate greater social and political awareness. In the interests of their immigrant and other clients, they will also need to question social policy, social priorities, the allocation of resources, and the quality of the social services; to speak out more clearly on racial discrimination and on immigration policies which split up families, disperse children from their traditional community, or deny basic human rights. Such an approach should lead to the location of many social problems in the social structure—their proper context—rather than in the clients' personalities.

Under the recent Immigration Bill, for instance, which had its third reading at the time of writing, if the head of a family is deported then the rest of the family will also have to leave the U.K. Also suppose that you are a respectable adult British subject who happened to arrive here from India many years ago as a child; and suppose that when you arrived your uncle pretended—without your quite understanding what was going on—to be your father. Under the Immigration Bill you can be deported any time this 'false declaration' is discovered and you have no right to appeal.

There are other areas of social and psychological need, at both a family and community level, which are appropriately within the social worker's function. However, for the worker to be accepted and to be in a position to decide the when, where, and how of the helping process, it is necessary for him to identify with the immigrants' situation, grasp the special features of their cultural system, and understand their current situation. This understanding must go well beyond intellectual identification and the collection of information; it must involve the worker's emotions. A further point stressed by Fantl and Meyer[1] is the necessity of understanding the impact of the client's milieu on his functioning to avoid confusing psychopathology with reactions to stress and conflicts in the life situation, and to permit diagnosis and treatment that are determined individually rather than by generalities. Similarly, an assessment of personality problems must involve the social worker in identifying the cultural features of behaviour and how culture and personality interact. Obviously, the dynamics of a situation can be more easily grasped when client and worker share a common cultural background which is experienced and understood by both. White social workers, however, have their own value orientations which can make it difficult for them to respond in ways that are meaningful to their immigrant clients. These orientations may involve approaches to various life situations that differ from those of the client, and eventually the workers can easily find themselves at odds with the expectations of their coloured clients.

[1] B. Fantl, 'Casework in Lower Class Districts', *Mental Hygiene* (Vol. 40, July 1961), pp. 425–38. C. H. Meyer, 'Individualizing the Multi-Problem Family', *Social Casework* (Vol. 40, No. 5, May 1963), pp. 267–72.

One important question that arises from this is how far white social workers, reared and shaped in the values of their own culture, can understand and help clients from diametrically opposite orientations. Social work experience, however, suggests that mature people are usually able to play a multiplicity of roles and express a broad spectrum of feelings. The effectiveness of their intervention will, nevertheless, be directly related to the degree of their appreciation of the special features of their clients' socio-cultural and psychological background and their responsiveness to it. This appreciation should enable white social workers to appraise strengths and the degree of healthy personal and social functioning in their clients. At this stage it is interesting to point to similar preoccupations among educationalists regarding the educational assessment of immigrant children. Educationalists now realize that the theory and practice of many techniques used to assess the educational progress of immigrant children are based on inadequate and sometimes outdated ideas and beliefs. A report recently produced for the Department of Education and Science recommended that 'consideration should be given to the wider dissemination of information about current concepts of intellectual development, about social, cultural and linguistic factors in individual growth and about the evaluation of educational progress'.[1]

The establishment of a helping relationship is difficult enough with most clients without the added factor of colour. When the worker and client are from different cultural backgrounds, the possibilities for misperception and miscommunication are infinitely greater. Clients often emotionally, if not intellectually, resist attempts aimed at helping them, but when the worker and the clients are also members of different racial groups the factor of race or colour, and of colour prejudice and discrimination, cannot be side-stepped. Curry[2] comments that when the variable of colour is added to the social work relationship, it seems to function like a Rorschach card capable of stimulating a wide range of reactions that

[1] Department of Education and Science, *Potential and Progress in a Second Culture* (London, H.M.S.O., 1971). (Education Survey, No. 10.)

[2] A. E. Curry, 'The Negro Worker and the White Client: A Commentary on the Treatment Relationship', *Social Casework* (Vol. 40, No. 3, March 1964), pp. 131–6.

indicate the underlying emotional frame of mind of the helper and the person helped. White social workers obviously cannot avoid acknowledging the difference in colour and race between them and their coloured clients, and it is honest to discuss its possible implications. For both the worker and the client it is an opportunity for an honest examination of their values and prejudices that are likely to affect the establishment of positive contact. We know, for instance, that white patients in hospital are often hostile to coloured doctors or nurses, tending to underestimate their ability and authority. On the other hand, many black clients accept too easily the authority of white people. This acceptance may blind social workers to the reality or strength of the underlying feeling—which can often amount to real fury. The process of acknowledging differences will easily falter, however, if it simply focuses on highlighting or stressing the difference between black and white, making the former feel even more separate and different. There have been situations when coloured clients have rejected the coloured social workers assigned to them because it seemed to these clients that they were being singled out from the rest of the community and thus made to feel different.

A further difficulty—which has led to a failure to offer immigrant clients an effective social work service—has been the social workers' tendency to attach more importance to psychopathology and the psychodynamics of personality than to socio-cultural and environmental factors. There is the suggestion that social workers may tend to apply methods that are not always relevant to their clients' conditions either because they feel more comfortable with such methods or because these methods have been unjustifiably labelled as 'advanced'. The preoccupation of many social workers, especially in the fifties and early sixties, with 'psychiatric' methods led to the rejection of non-permissive techniques and to the location of most problems in the individual, with little regard to social, cultural, and economic circumstances. As a result, large numbers of clients were dropped as 'unhelpable' or described as hard-to-reach because they would not respond to methods that were more appropriate to mainly neurotic or middle-class clients with either a higher level of integration or some apparent 'sophistication'. Permissive, non-directive, interpretive techniques generally aim at developing 'insight' and self-direction in clients and involve intra-psychic processes based mostly on verbal communication. Immigrants, who are not introspectively inclined, were among the group of clients whose needs were lost sight of by some sections of the social work profession. The non-directive approach and the formality surrounding techniques of exploring under-lying feeling are alien to the experiences of most immigrants. As a helping method it is generally outside their comprehen-sion and irrelevant to both their predominantly social and personal needs.

Experience suggests that immigrant clients expect their social workers to be more open and less subtle in their com-munications and to be willing to take the initiative or point out consequences. They expect them to be more active in helping them to obtain necessary services and resources and, where appropriate, to act as their spokesmen and to represent them on tribunals, committees, and so on. Fears of depen-dency at this stage are unjustified in the face of real need which cannot be met by the efforts of the immigrants alone. The eventual aim should be to help immigrants to be more independent and speak for themselves. They should also be encouraged to play a greater social and political part in shap-ing their future. Immigrants, as a rule, are more likely to respond to measures aimed at alleviating pressing social needs and anxieties arising from current pressures rather than to efforts to involve them in introspective considerations. In other words, the problems of most immigrants have more to do with real, everyday situations and are less the result of distortions from within.

It would of course be naïve to maintain that immigrants do not have both inner and outer needs. When there are inner needs these are likely to be masked by an overlay of material difficulties. The way to help this latter group is, however, again, to respond to their social needs before trying to reach their personal ones. Through the demonstration of interest and concern in a form that is meaningful to them, trust can be established within which personal problems may later be discussed. Though social work literature has appropriately demonstrated how certain practical difficulties can be resolved by focusing on the personal problems that generate them, less importance has been paid to the equally important fact that some personal problems can be resolved through the manipulation of the environment. Social work as a helping process has inherent flexibility which has not yet been utilized to its full effect. The situation presented by the presence of many immigrants has exposed not only the limited range of knowledge used in evaluation and assessment of immigrant clients, but also the limited range of methods and skills utilized in the helping process with local clients.

The suggestion has also been made that because immigrants are used to the pattern of living associated with extended families and because privacy among them is less valued, they would respond well to group work methods. The operation of most groups, at any rate as currently fantasied by many social workers, involves yet again processes aimed at exposing underlying feeling and undervalues the potentiality for 'advice or information giving or of exercising necessary controls'. Group procedures related to exposing underlying feeling would be as alien and unproductive with immigrant clients as the predominantly non-directive intensive casework methods discussed earlier. A pattern is now developing in group work, as it did before with casework, of specific procedures being again used without relating them to assessment and aims. This unsatisfactory situation is likely to continue until the nature of social work is clarified and based on firm social work practice principles independent of other disciplines.

Final Conclusion

The contributions in this publication are based mainly on observations from practice and are quoted as a general guide. There is a certain danger of stereotyping all immigrants from the same ethnic group as being the same, irrespective of their sub-cultural group and of their individual circumstances. Fibush[1] appropriately warns that 'even when a sociocultural

[1] F. Fibush, 'The White Worker and the Negro Client', *Social Casework* (Vol. 46, No. 5, May 1965), pp. 271–7.

condition applies to all members of a group, its impact will vary according to the individual's unique endowment, developmental history and environmental circumstances'.

It is proper that observations from practice should be tested and examined further if they are to serve as guides to social work practice. There is a dearth of studies about immigrants and their way of life. One area for research which is of particular interest to social workers is the mutual perception of immigrant client and social worker and the way it affects the social work relationship. Another area is the impact of change on the immigrants' values, for example, the effect which immigration has on the structure and functioning of the family. To what extent does the personality sustain its identity in the process of change and often in the face of considerable pressures and open hostility? It is equally important to learn how African and other coloured children fostered by white people, fare in later life after returning to their original homes or countries and how this experience affects their personal identity. In the meantime, and until such studies are made available, the practitioner has to do something.

Social work courses have a responsibility not only to ensure that socio-cultural and economic factors are not neglected but also to teach the special features of social work with immigrants. Whilst it is appropriate to concentrate teaching on the generic nature of social work theory and practice, it is the identification of special and unique features in each case or situation that will continue to give real meaning to the social work principle of 'individualizing'. To ignore the teaching of cultural patterns and of current reality stresses faced by immigrants might lead newly qualified workers to assume the existence or absence of need, deviance, or illness, and so to fail to provide a service. The social worker's job in general could be made easier if the need for more specialized information on immigrants were acknowledged, so that its systematic collection and development could start. The pressing need is for a kind of resource bank of cultural information and some guidance about its implication for social work practice. Social workers could then draw on this resource bank for their day-to-day work.

Select Bibliography

Bernstein, B., 'A socio-linguistic approach to social learning', in Gould, J. (ed.), *Penguin survey of the social sciences*. Harmondsworth, Penguin, 1965.

Burney, E., *Housing on trial*. London, Oxford University Press, for Institute of Race Relations, 1967.

Butterworth, E., and Kinnisburgh, D., *The social background of immigrant children from India, Pakistan and Cyprus*. London, Books for Schools, 1970.

Coard, B., *How the West Indian child is made educationally subnormal in the British school system*. London, New Beacon Books, 1971.

Daniel, W. W., *Racial discrimination in England*. Harmondsworth, Penguin, 1969.

Davison, R. B., *Black British*. Oxford University Press, for Institute of Race Relations, 1966.

Eversley, D., and Sukdeo, F., *The dependants of the coloured Commonwealth population of England and Wales*. London, Institute of Race Relations Special Series, 1969.

Fitzherbert, K., *West Indian children in London*. London, Bell, 1967.

Hashmi, F., *Immigration and medical and social aspects*. London, Churchill Ltd., 1966.

Hashmi, F., *The Pakistani family in Britain*. London, National Committee for Commonwealth Immigrants, 1967.

Hiro, D., *The Indian family in Britain*. London, National Committee for Commonwealth Immigrants, 1967.

Humphry, D., and John, G., *Because they are black*. Harmondsworth, Penguin, 1971.

International Social Service, *Immigrants at London Airport and their settlement in the community*. London, I.S.S., June 1967.

Jones, K., and Smith, A. D., *The economic impact of Commonwealth immigration*. London, Cambridge University Press, for National Institute of Economic and Social Research, 1970.

John, A., *et al.*, *Race in the inner city: a report from Handsworth, Birmingham*. London, Runnymede Trust, 1970.

Oakley, R., *New backgrounds: the immigrant child at home and at school*. London, Oxford University Press, for Institute of Race Relations, 1968.

Political and Economic Planning and Research Services Ltd., *Racial discrimination*. London, P.E.P., 1967.

Raynor, L., *Adoption of non-white children*. London, Allen & Unwin, 1970.

Rees, T., *Policy or drift*. London, Runnymede Trust, 1971.

Rex, J., and Moore, R., *Race, community, and conflict*. London, Oxford University Press, for Institute of Race Relations, 1969.

Rose, E. J. B., *et al.*, *Colour and citizenship: a report on British race relations*. London, Oxford University Press, for Institute of Race Relations, 1969.

Sharma, U., *Rampal and his family: the story of an immigrant*. London, Collins, 1971.

Youth Service Development Council Committee, *Immigrants and the youth service*. London, H.M.S.O., 1967. Chairman: Lord Hunt.

Articles

Alam, M. N., 'English and Indian maladjusted boys'. *Case conference*, Vol. 14, No. 1, May 1967.

Curry, A. E., 'The Negro worker and the white client: a commentary on the treatment relationship'. *Social casework*, Vol. 40, March 1964.

Fibush, F., 'The white worker and the Negro client'. *Social casework*, Vol. 46, May 1965.

Foren, R., and Batta, I. D., 'Colour as a variable in the use made of a local authority child care department'. *Social work*, Vol. 27, No. 3, July 1970.

Hashmi, F., 'Psychology of racial prejudice'. *Alta*, the University of Birmingham Review, Winter 1967–8.

Holman, R., 'Immigrants and child care policy'. *Case conference*, Vol. 15, No. 7, November 1968.

Price, J. R., 'West Indian immigrants: assimilation and casework'. *Case conference*, Vol. 12, No. 2, June 1965.

Shapiro, P., 'Illegitimate coloured children in long-term care'. *Case conference*, Vol. 15, No. 1, May 1968.

Stewart-Prince, G., 'Emotional problems of children reunited with their migrant families in Britain'. *Maternal and child care*, December 1968.

Triseliotis, J. P., 'Immigrant schoolchildren and their problem of adjustment'. *Case conference*, Vol. 9, No. 7, January 1963.

Triseliotis, J. P., 'Casework with immigrants: the implications of cultural factors'. *The British journal of psychiatric social work*, Vol. 8, 1965.

Walker, A., 'Social influences on disturbed immigrant children'. *Case conference*, Vol. 15, No. 6, October 1968.

Other Sources of Relevant Literature

Social workers will find the publications of the following groups particularly relevant:

The Community Relations Commission
   Russell Square House
   10/12 Russell Square
   London, W.C.1

The Runnymede Trust
   2 Arundel Street
   London, W.C.2

The Institute of Race Relations
   36 Jermyn Street
   London, S.W.1

The Institute regularly produces two publications:
   Race Today, a monthly, contains discussion of recent developments, reports, articles, and book reviews. It focuses mainly upon Britain.
   Race, a quarterly journal, is more academic in approach and more international in coverage.

Other bodies which produce material of relevance to social workers include:
   The British Council of Churches' Community and Race Relations Unit
   The Catholic Institute for International Relations
   Christian Action
   The Commonwealth Institute
   The National Council for Civil Liberties
   The Race Relations Committee of the Society of Friends
   The United Nations Association

DATE DUE
